ENDORSEMENTS

Breakthrough Faith by Larry Sparks is clearly written from a pure heart and a compassionate desire to bring the reader into more of God. Whether hungry for revival or wondering if God's Holy Spirit is still being poured out today, readers will find their hearts gently opened to discover that there is indeed more. Larry has done a great job of laying out how to come into "greater works" and see God bring breakthrough faith to operate in and through our lives.

BILL JOHNSON
Senior Leader of Bethel Church, Redding, California
Author of *When Heaven Invades Earth* and *Hosting the Presence*

Larry Sparks's new book *Breakthrough Faith* is a powerful book. He provides a solid biblical basis for the activation of faith and how to sustain it. He helps the reader come to an understanding of the faith God has already given them in salvation. I really appreciated the insights into an understanding of sovereignty that causes everything in our lives to be the will of God. Instead of a blueprint worldview, he understands the dynamics of a worldview that includes warfare between the devil and his demons and Jesus, His church, and the angels.

The insight that faith comes as a gift from God is important for our day. We don't need to get more faith; it's discovering what we have already received and to start putting it to work. He sees three important aspects of faith: one, the importance of declarations rooted in the truth of God and God's *rhema* words; two, the importance of the testimony to faith; and three, an understanding of the nearness of the Presence of God in our lives. The importance of perseverance is highlighted throughout the book as well as a way to activate faith to get the breakthrough. *Breakthrough Faith* is an important book on one of the most important subjects in the entire Bible. A great read.

DR. RANDY CLARK
Founder and President, Global Awakening
Author of *There is More* and co-author of *Essential Guide to Healing*

Larry Sparks is a young man of vision and promise. I met him in the classroom at Regent University and found him to be a very good student. I am not surprised that he has written such an excellent book. *Breakthrough Faith* is a positive message for us all to live a more active life of faith in our day. Well done, Larry!

DR. VINSON SYNAN
Dean Emeritus of the Regent University School of Divinity
Virginia Beach, Virginia
Author of *The Century of the Holy Spirit*

Breakthrough Faith equips you with practical yet powerful keys on how to exercise your faith and walk in the miraculous as a lifestyle. The men and women God has used throughout history to accomplish great things were not extraordinary individuals. Often, they had many odds against them. One common denominator that positioned all of God's generals to be history makers in their respective generations was how they stewarded and released their faith.

In this exciting new book, Larry Sparks invites you to consider the powerful inheritance you received when you gave your life to Jesus Christ—*faith*. The very faith that broke through your old life, saving you from sin, is the same faith that empowers you to walk in God's supernatural power today.

Signs, wonders, and miracles were never meant to be here-and-there occurrences. These are the very things that Jesus said would follow those who believe, those who exercise faith in Him. *Breakthrough Faith* takes you on a life-changing journey that will transform the way you see faith *forever*.

DR. ROBERTS LIARDON
International Speaker
Author of the bestselling *God's Generals* series and *Visions of Heaven*

Larry Sparks's book *Breakthrough Faith* is a timely and empowering message for God's people. He captures the very principle that sustained me through the darkest and most difficult season of my life: faith that perseveres and breaks through every obstacle experiences God's promises.

For anyone who is facing impossible circumstances, Larry's book will encourage you to keep pressing on. Only the supernatural power of faith can help you overcome the odds and break through the boundaries that separate you from your miracle. This work provides a powerful perspective on the topic of faith that hands you the keys to put into action the miraculous faith that is your inheritance as a believer.

JORDAN RUBIN, NMD, PhD
Founder, Garden of Life and Beyond Organic
New York Times bestselling author of *The Maker's Diet*

As a personal friend, I can testify that Larry Sparks's heart burns for revival. I believe these pages release an impartation of that very fire. *Breakthrough Faith* is your scripturally based user's guide on how to practically live *revival* as an everyday lifestyle. In this book, Larry reveals how faith is your secret to walking in this sustained, continuous flow of God's supernatural Presence and power.

I know that there are many books on faith, but I am confident that *Breakthrough Faith* will lead you into a deeper encounter with the Person of Jesus Christ and increase your passion for His Presence.

PASTOR DARREN DAVIS
Senior Leader, The Harbour Church
Fort Lauderdale, Florida

Here is good news! In an excellent way, Larry Sparks has removed much of the theological insulation that handicaps our concept of faith. He peels away huge layers of the mystery and enables us to examine the subject much more objectively.

You will find his writing to be conversational and easy to grasp. It is calculated but uncomplicated. I am now in my sixty-fifth year of ordained ministry and the message was an eye-opener to me. My only regret is that I did not have its benefit years ago. This book will help push all of us into our "breakthrough."

CHARLES CARRIN
Keynote speaker with R.T. Kendall and Jack Taylor
for "Word, Spirit, and Power" conferences
Author of *Edge of Glory* and co-author of *Word, Spirit, Power*

Larry's book *Breakthrough Faith* is a powerful book equipping the saints to embrace the faith they have in them through the Presence of the Holy Spirit. I truly believe God calls us to live an abundant life that is only possible as we rise up in faith and obedience. I know this book will encourage you to break through for victory in your life.

TOM MULLINS
Founding Pastor, Christ Fellowship Church
Author of *The Leadership Game* and *The Confidence Factor*

The same faith in Christ by which we are saved is the faith that helps us live in freedom and victory today. *Breakthrough Faith* challenges us to boldly step out with confidence in God and expect Him to boldly show up in our lives. Larry Sparks is a brother in Christ and a friend, and God has given him a word that will encourage you in your faith.

TODD MULLINS
Lead Pastor, Christ Fellowship Church

For many of my believing patients, worry, anxiety, and fear are constant companions: fear of death, fear of danger, fear of disease. All too often, these fears are crippling, keeping us from the life God has called us to live. But it doesn't have to be that way. Larry Sparks's new book *Breakthrough Faith* gives us the tools to become victorious in our faith as we walk through the battles of life. This book is essential for those who are both new to the faith and mature in Christ.

CHAUNCEY CRANDALL, MD
Director of Preventive Medicine and Cardiology
Palm Beach Cardiovascular Clinic
Evangelist, Christ for All Nations with Reinhard Bonnke

It's been said that every challenge you encounter in life is a fork in the road. You have the choice to choose which way to go—backward, forward, breakdown, or breakthrough. *Breakthrough Faith* is a God-breathed treatise on how to meet the challenge and get Heaven's desired results. Larry has done an awesome job identifying the obstacles and opposition to activating real faith, and he has laid out a blueprint for achieving victory and occupying new territories. I recommend this book for every believer who wants to go to the next level.

SEAN SMITH

Evangelist, Sean Smith Ministries/Pointblank International
Author of *I Am Your Sign* and *Prophetic Evangelism*

Breakthrough Faith invites you to know and worship God in a deeper way. Larry Sparks in an encourager and his writing will inspire you to live the life in Christ that you were destined for.

MICHAEL NEALE

Worship leader, recording artist, and national bestselling author of
The River and co-writer of "Your Great Name"

If you are ready to be empowered with tools that will launch you in achieving your desires and destiny, then you need to read *Breakthrough Faith*! Larry lays out profound principles that will take you from where you are to where you have dreamed of being. Unlocking the keys to living and thriving in a lifestyle of faith is essential to receiving all that God has for you. This book will definitely do that for you as you apply its principles. I highly recommend this book! It will change your life forever.

MICHAEL KAYLOR

Conference Speaker and Pastor
Author of *The Adventure of Supernatural Discovery*

The Christian life cannot exist without a tenacious faith to lay hold of the promises of God. Each of us must learn to live on a Word, even when we don't immediately see its fulfillment. Larry Sparks captures that lifestyle of audacious faith so well in *Breakthrough Faith*. He teaches us that we can and must overcome the onslaught of the enemy as we simply believe God. Larry inspires us to never settle until we see the miraculous invade our lives. Let this book awaken you into a supernatural lifestyle where nothing is impossible with God.

Karen Wheaton
Founder and Senior Leader of The Ramp

Larry Sparks, a gifted communicator and intuitive observer of our human experience, has presented a brilliant treatise on the subject of Faith. His personal relationship with God is evidenced in his writing.

When facts try to diminish your sensibility to believe in a favorable outcome to your prayers, reading this book will encourage you to maintain your faith in God in spite of circumstances and situations. With faith in God all things are indeed possible. With faith in God you can mount up over your problems like an eagle, because your faith will give you wings.

Dr. Cindy Trimm
Bestselling Author, Minister, Life-Strategist

You haven't read enough books on faith until you read Larry Sparks' Breakthrough Faith. With solid theology and practical experience, Larry answers questions about faith that many are afraid to ask while also equipping and inspiring you to exercise your faith to walk in a supernatural lifestyle where anything is possible. Every Christian needs to read this book.

Jennifer LeClaire
Author and Senior Editor, *Charisma* magazine
Director, Awakening House of Prayer in Fort Lauderdale

In *Breakthrough Faith,* Larry equips the reader with the tools needed to see a breakthrough of epic proportions. These time-tested truths will propel you into a new level of faith to believe God for the impossible."

Sid Roth
Host, *It's Supernatural*

BREAKTHROUGH FAITH

BREAKTHROUGH FAITH

LIVING A LIFE WHERE ANYTHING IS POSSIBLE

LARRY SPARKS

DESTINY IMAGE® PUBLISHERS, INC.

P.O. Box 310, Shippensburg, PA 17257-0310

"Promoting Inspired Lives."

This book and all other Destiny Image, Revival Press, MercyPlace, Fresh Bread, Destiny Image Fiction, and Treasure House books are available at Christian bookstores and distributors worldwide.

For more information on foreign distributors, call 717-532-3040.

Reach us on the Internet: www.destinyimage.com.

ISBN 13 TP: 978-0-7684-0451-7

ISBN 13 Ebook: 978-0-7684-0452-4

For Worldwide Distribution, Printed in the U.S.A.

2 3 4 5 6 7 8 / 18 17 16 15

DEDICATION

Breakthrough Faith is dedicated to my beautiful wife, Mercedes. Without you this project would not have taken shape. In fact, without you this entire journey would not be what it is today. I am thoroughly convinced that when it came to my spouse and life partner, God strategically put me with the one who would call out the gold inside of me, speak to my destiny, and make what was impossible on my own become possible as a couple, as one flesh.

Greater love has no one than this, than to lay down one's life for his friends (John 15:13).

You have demonstrated this Christlike love time after time in our marriage as you have laid down your life for me, our family, and the call of God on our lives. For modeling breakthrough faith when I have not and for being a living embodiment of what this book is all about—I am forever grateful, appreciative, and awed at God for bringing our lives together.

And to my precious daughter, Liberty—what many are now presenting in words will be what you experience and enjoy as a lifestyle. May you go higher, deeper, and further than my generation ever dreamed possible.

ACKNOWLEDGMENTS

My favorite works, from art and literature to music and film, are those expressions that were born out of experience. Such projects are not thrown together haphazardly, nor are the authors passionate to steward their creation just to bring in a quick buck. They were hit with something and could not function as normal until that "something" was captured through their unique medium of creativity.

In the Kingdom of God, my favorite books, music, and sermons are those birthed out of the place of encounter with God. Such is *Breakthrough Faith*. Even though it has only taken months to put these words into a document, the journey of this message has been at least ten years in the making—and still ongoing even as I write.

I do not dare claim to be some final authority on the topic of faith. Not even close. There are several incredible works on the subject that have been absolutely instrumental in building my personal understanding of what faith is and how it is expressed. All I know is that it was God's perfect time for me to share these thoughts with you. So my humble prayer is that beyond mere information or even inspiration, you would encounter the Presence and Person of Jesus Christ throughout these pages.

I cannot continue without extending brief acknowledgment to those who were vital in helping me bring this work to fruition. After all, the work and the worker are vitally interconnected. Those who invested in my personal journey with God have, in turn, invested into the unfolding of this project.

To my mentors, both far and near: Pastor Bill Johnson, you continue to inspire me through your humility and hunger for God. Your lifestyle of risk is what has paved the way for me to receive and carry a message like this. And the most incredible thing is that the supernatural culture you are sowing into at Bethel is one powerful example that makes the message of *Breakthrough Faith* possible for believers to embrace as a sustained lifestyle. You witness it on a daily basis.

Pastor Todd Mullins, God strategically placed you in my life back in 1999 to be a mentor, a dear brother in Christ, and an example of great integrity. I know how busy your schedule has been over the years, so know full well that every lunch, word of encouragement, and meeting you have so graciously invested into me has been key in cultivating this message of breakthrough faith.

And to Pastor Tom Mullins, I have had the great honor of calling both you and Todd my pastors since July of 1999. It was during this time that I had an encounter with the Holy Spirit (at a Saturday night service over at the South Campus) where I was left with no other option but to surrender everything to Jesus. A million "thank yous" for continuing to faithfully host His Presence until this very day. All it took was that one meeting with God, and everything changed.

To my family: Mom and Dad, you truly had ears tuned into Heaven when you enrolled me in Holy Spirit Catholic School back in 1988, and I'm continually grateful that I am still getting a tremendous education in "Holy Spirit school" every day of my life. Know that because of your continuous support and encouragement, I am able to pursue the vision God has placed in my heart.

To my Destiny Image family: Ronda and Nathan, words cannot express how overwhelmed I am at your belief, your support, your encouragement, and your willingness to get this message out. Mykela, you have been instrumental in this process—without you, this work would not have gotten finished and would not be in print! You, along with the entire Destiny Image team, carry an incredible mandate from Heaven to declare the uncompromised, due season word of the Lord. It is an absolute privilege to be part of a company that has published so many of the trailblazers and pioneers that have invested in my life.

To my dear friends: Andrew, Kyle, and Caleb. In chapter 24 I wrote with the three of you in mind as I described "faith friends" who have the desire for the impossible etched into their very DNA. The gift of your friendship is truly priceless. How many people can you talk to about *anything* and, without strain or difficulty, transition right into celebrating the greatness and limitlessness of God? Caleb, even though you are no longer with us on the earth, I know your view of God's world is mind-blowing. You constantly see what is available in Heaven and are always cheering us on to make withdrawals from God's limitless supply.

Finally, to those of you who have sown into my life over the past ten years as this message was being cultivated within me: you do not merely speak or write nice words. What you speak and what you write carries the very power of God to bring about supernatural transformation. I am always inspired by how your lives consistently represent King Jesus and demonstrate His Kingdom. To Jack Hayford, Karen Wheaton, Darlene Zschech, Reinhard Bonnke, Randy Clark, Sid Roth, Corey Russell, John Bevere, Joyce Meyer, Mike Bickle, Dr. Michael Brown, David Sprague, Vinson Synan, R.T. Kendall, Jack Taylor, the Adrian Rogers Family, Allen Hood, Chauncey Crandall, John Piper, and the countless others I have surely missed.

Dear Reader: May the words shared in the following pages give you license to pursue and experience everything God has made available for you in the Lord Jesus Christ.

~~

We are not waiting for Heaven to release a new level of faith to the church. Rather, Heaven is waiting for the people of God to awaken to what they already received at salvation and start living like the inheritance of faith they received in Christ is actually able to move mountains, break through impossibilities, and bring the Kingdom of God to earth. Breakthrough faith is not unusual; it is normal. My prayer is that you, dear reader, would be led by the Holy Spirit and tutored by the Word of God as you discover how to live out this new "normal" using the pages ahead.

~~

CONTENTS

FOREWORD

Why write another book on faith? After all, isn't faith about the most discussed, debated, and referred-to subject in Scripture? Doesn't about everybody have a working knowledge of the subject of faith? My answer to my own questions is this: no subject runs a greater risk of being misunderstood, taken for granted, or downright misused as the most familiar ones. The fact that we all can say the word does not guarantee that we know or understand the meaning of that word. Thus, every now and then there needs to be a fresh breath of open evaluation and discussion of what we have all too often taken for granted.

This is the best reason I can think of for another book on faith, at least a book like this one! I have walked through this book, trying to live out its contents, and am left with the feeling that a fresh wind has blown upon my soul. Such a breeze is welcome, especially in times of ease when all seems well, but when in fact there is an erosion taking place in our understanding of the great subjects of Christianity. So with a crafty pen and a keen mind, Larry Sparks has presented to us a table laden with "vital victuals" for the hungry and the hurting on a subject at the heart of our expectations.

I have personally been involved lately in reexamining the issue of faith and am amazed at how quickly I began to learn things that brought this topic alive for me. However faith is defined, described, or valued, it has a "breakthrough" quality inherit within it. Years ago a friend of mine who is now in Heaven used to say, "The foundation of faith is antagonism." The rightness of this statement seems more right and relevant with the passing of years. This book is well named and is much needed in our unique moment in history. The word on my mind for the current year, which, at this writing, began a few days ago, is "breakthrough." I know more people, businesses, churches, nations, and regions for whom a breakthrough of miraculous magnitude is a mandate, not just a hope or a choice.

In my estimation, this book helps us believe that a breakthrough of epic proportions is pending for every reader. This is a sweeping statement, but I have often found myself thinking, "Larry has left no stone unturned on the issue of faith and revitalization that will attend this study." God has let us know that without faith it is impossible to please Him, so with the realization that God is well pleased with faith, we should plunge into this study with great interest and expectation.

The reading of this book is apt to bring us into untold and unimagined levels of increasing faith and quality ministry. The faith we seek is God's faith, not ours. Our best human faith is flawed from the beginning. Paul said it better than I ever could in his summary statement that nothing matters *"but faith working through love"* (Gal. 5:6). Faith, when it is fueled by love, is never static.

This volume stirs our faith, demonstrating what Paul meant when he said, *"The righteousness of God is revealed from faith to faith"* (Rom. 1:17). Happy reading! You are holding in your hand a great book on faith!

JACK TAYLOR
President, Dimensions Ministries, Melbourne, Florida
Co-author of *Word, Spirit, Power*

Preface

OPEN UP THE GATES

In 2012, I had a vision that changed my life forever. During a revival service in Orlando, FL the presence of God invaded that church sanctuary in such a strong, tangible way that, towards the end of the meeting, I went running up to the altar. Many of us did. It was not an invitation for people to receive healing, a miracle, or some other kind of breakthrough. The call was extended to those who were hungry for God. At the time, my mind could not completely wrap around what was happening—I just knew God was powerfully at work.

I thought I was relatively hungry for God... until His presence touched me afresh. That night, I was reminded of how every touch from Heaven escorts us into new levels of hunger for God and encounter with God. Why? Because every time you are touched by God's presence, you are reminded of how great He is. You are reintroduced anew to the limitless expanse of Who He is. There is always more of God to experience simply because of His size and scope. Our God is not small. He is not containable. He is Almighty and unlimited. There are vast canyons of His glory and un-scalable heights of His majesty that our mortal minds have not even conceived of, let alone mastered. Suffice it to say, the Holy Spirit was up to something significant in these powerful moments. Little did I know *how* significant this encounter would be.

The worship leader, Lydia Stanley Marrow, started leading the congregation in a prophetic song. Over and over, she sang the words: *open up the gates, open up the doors.* Every time she made this declaration, it was like the hunger level in the room escalated. Something was happening in the spirit realm as the people became visibly desperate for God. Even though I had experienced a certain measure of God's presence in my life, this encounter ignited fresh fire within me. I was reminded of God's greatness and how much *more* of Him there was to experience.

As Lydia sang, I started to have a vision of the mind. I had this mental picture of an old, rusty gate—kind of like something you would see leading into a castle. It was not a door, but rather, a gate with iron bars reaching from top to bottom. The interesting thing about this gate was its response to the congregation's united cry of hunger. Hunger was actually the key to making the gate open up. In fact, the word "open" doesn't do the picture justice. Hunger caused the gate to rise and lift up incrementally. It rose up from the ground, providing a greater level of access from one side of the gate to the next. The outside light was able to come in *through* the gate in an increased measure as it lifted up.

Then, I started to understand what was happening and the revelation the Holy Spirit was releasing.

As a student of revival history, the one thing I have learned is this— God's power has never been withdrawn from the earth. If anyone tries to convince you that there have been *times and seasons* of God's power— where He made a sovereign decision to pour it out and then withdraw it—you are dealing with incorrect theology that cripples spiritual hunger. There was one Day of Pentecost and one outpouring of the Holy Spirit. This took place roughly two thousand years ago. We don't need another outpouring of the Spirit from Heaven; I believe Heaven is waiting for an outpouring of *hunger* from the Earth.

This is not a call to strive, labor, beg, barter and plead with God. Far from it. It's an invitation to experience God afresh by going into His Word and simply asking Him, *What is your standard for the normal Christian life?* I want to live in agreement with God's standard. Not the standard of a denomination, pastor, ideology, parent, or perspective. If these people and ideas are in agreement with Scripture, wonderful! If they are not, I must uphold God's Word no matter what. His Word is the definitive standard for what I am licensed to believe God for this side of eternity.

We are living at a unique moment in history where it's no longer just scattered individuals who are living this kind of breakthrough lifestyle; entire church communities are walking in God's miraculous power… and it's becoming *normal*, not the exception. From Pentecost until today, there have been men and women throughout the centuries who have pressed into the fullness of God and experienced supernatural results. They made Scripture their standard for living. They saw Jesus Christ as the only example worth emulating. I would agree, these figures were few and far between throughout history—but they were undeniably present. As they tapped into the supernatural realm, it was like God's power was being released *through* those ancient gates in limited quantity.

Now, the gates are opening—and I believe in a greater measure than ever before. This is not necessarily God's sovereignty; it is a corporate cry that resounds, *God, there must be more! I want everything Your Word promises. That is my standard for living.* People are becoming less content with doing comfortable Christianity and are becoming desperate to carry the Kingdom of God into their everyday lives. As our hunger level increases, the gates will fling open wider than ever before.

That night at the revival meeting, I envisioned those gates rising in such a dramatic way that the body of Christ began to experience an unrestricted flow of supernatural power, from Heaven to Earth. This is where we are headed as the church and this is why I believe the message of *Breakthrough Faith* is truly "due season."

Get ready to experience a fresh touch from God in every area of your life and become a catalyst through which the Holy Spirit can release His supernatural power. Truly, this is the key to fulfilling your life purpose and changing the world!

INTRODUCTION

This was their chance. Four friends had heard that this Man, Jesus, was coming to town. Now this Jesus was no ordinary teacher. Stories had been circulating around town, causing the people to buzz with anticipation, expectation, intrigue, speculation, and even skepticism. Everyone wanted to catch a glimpse of Him. People wanted to come hear this Teacher who did not speak or teach as the Pharisees or religious leaders did, but delivered words of life with authority and power. It was as if He were a messenger from another world, another Kingdom altogether.

When He stepped onto the scene, miracles happened. Demons came out of people. Those who had leprosy were supernaturally healed and made clean. In fact, *everyone* who came to Jesus received miraculous healing from sickness and disease, as well as deliverance from demonic torment. Could it be that this Jesus would also extend a healing touch toward their paralyzed friend?

They started walking toward the house where they heard Jesus was teaching. Maybe along the way the four men told their paralyzed friend the stories they had heard about this Miracle Worker, building his faith and expectancy for the miracle they were all anticipating.

But then, there was a major obstacle. Jesus was there, teaching in the house. The problem was that the massive crowd made it impossible for the men to push their way through and bring their paralyzed friend to

Jesus. They could not even get near Him. The One who had the ability to bring a supernatural solution to their friend's impossible condition was just out of their reach. Would they experience a miracle, or go home the same way they came?

Two Options

Maybe this is just how you feel today—like Jesus is just out of your reach. Maybe your miracle feels out of reach. Or maybe you have been like these four friends and you are carrying someone else's burden, believing for their breakthrough, praying for their healing. But you have experienced roadblocks along the way. Setbacks keep pushing against your progress. The obstacles keep coming against you. Day by day the impossibility level rises. They call the disease terminal. The marriage is all but over. The anxiety is relentless. The thoughts of fear, terror, worry, lust, doubt, and anger just keep coming. The addiction is too strong and the grip of bondage is too tight.

You know that Jesus is able to do something about your situation. After all, He can do anything He wants—He is God. But the crowded house—the obstacle and seeming impossibility—causes you to wonder, "Jesus, I know You are able...but are You *willing*? I know You can transform my impossible situation, but do You want to?"

The four men were faced with a vital decision that we face every time we are confronted with the impossible. Option 1: they could embrace the crowded house as God's perfect will for their friend's life, assuming that because they could not easily get to Jesus, it was not His will to heal their paralyzed friend. This option embraces *everything* that happens in life as God's sovereign will and downplays the idea of pressing past impossibility to receive a supernatural solution.

If they selected this option, the four men would turn back, head home, and their friend would have remained in the same paralyzed condition perhaps for the rest of his life. Too many believers embrace this option today, not because it is theologically correct, but because it is all they have ever known. And plus, no one is providing a solid, scriptural alternative.

In the pages to come, I want to equip and empower you to live out the second option. As you will come to discover, these four men did not simply go with Option 1 and embrace the impossible situation as God's will. They demonstrated a completely different perspective, which I want to help you develop and activate. By the time you're finished reading this book, it is my hope that you would not only want to choose Option 2, but that it would be a way of life for you and your default option in every situation you face. By God's grace it is possible to look at our impossible situations with expectancy and faith.

MY MOTIVATION BEHIND THIS BOOK

I have watched many good, Jesus-loving, Bible-believing Christians simply embrace the circumstances life brings their way as God's will. Opposition. Overwhelming odds. Those things in life that are declared *terminal*. Sicknesses. Relationships. The spiritual climate of their family or city. When situations come against us that are considered terminal, our tendency is to embrace an experiential faith. We let the situation that comes against us *become* God's will instead of measuring it *beside* God's will. While there is mystery to God's will that we'll never know this side of Heaven, there is also clarity and revelation we are meant to understand now. God's Word reveals God's will concerning our lives. It is vital that we know what God's Word says about the different situations we experience because not everything that comes into our lives is God's perfect will for us.

I hear it time after time after time: someone is going through a difficult situation—be it an illness, a divorce, mental or emotional pain, family turmoil, or a continuous series of unfortunate events—and they are desperately searching for God's plan and purpose in all of it. Often, God's plan involves us overcoming the overwhelming thing that has come against our lives. We cannot afford to believe the lie that everything that happens in life is orchestrated by God's sovereign plan. He caused it. He orchestrated it. He set it up. He has a plan.

God absolutely has a good plan and a perfect purpose for each one of us, but it is quite different from the realities that so many Christians embrace and teach as His will. God's perfect will is actually on the *other side* of the barriers, impossibilities, and circumstances we mistakenly believe are sent from Him. His will is not simply embracing whatever comes our way. Instead, God's will invites us to experience His supernatural power invading impossibilities and overthrowing circumstances that do not agree with His perfect plan.

> **Not everything that comes into our lives is God's perfect will for us.**

What is the secret to experiencing and releasing this power in our lives? Breakthrough faith. I want to help you develop and unleash a personal faith that persists through every problem, perseveres through all circumstances, and breaks through every barrier that is in disagreement with God's Word.

WORD OF FAITH?

My journey with faith has been interesting, as you will soon discover. One thing I *do not* want to do is discourage anyone from pressing in for breakthrough using *all* of the incredible tools that are available.

Even though I will talk about some of the imbalances, misuses and abuses of certain faith-related teachings, I do believe there are valuable treasures in what is commonly called the *Word of Faith* movement. Yes, there have been those who have taken positive confession to ludicrous extremes, thus producing a carnal prosperity message and hyper "name it, claim it" theology. I want to challenge you—don't throw the baby out with the bathwater. Excess does not give you or I the license to say, "That teaching is heretical!" and completely write it off.

Does this mean that the original, foundational teaching is wrong? No. Every movement and its corresponding doctrine has its deviations. Every truth has its counterfeits. Just because counterfeit $20 bills exist, this does not mean that we should throw away *all* $20 bills. To recognize the counterfeit, we study the original.

The same is true with Word of Faith theology. The body of Christ can profoundly benefit from many of its Bible-based principles. One, it keeps us speaking Scripture, no matter what comes against us. Two, it encourages us to exalt the Word of God over any impossibility or obstacle. Three, it keeps us mindful of *who* we are agreeing with—God, our circumstances or the devil. Four, it renews our minds and changes our vocabulary to reflect God's speech.

Perhaps the greatest contribution of the Word of Faith movement is the emphasis on practically applying Scripture to everyday life situations. The Bible is not merely a book to be read; it is a confession to be declared in both our words and lifestyles. It's not enough to just believe the Bible; we need to put what we believe into practice. The demons *believe* in one God and tremble. What makes us different?

> *Since we have the same spirit of faith according to what has been written, "I believed, and so I spoke," we also believe, and so we also speak.* (2 Corinthians 4:13, ESV)

Breakthrough Faith is all about putting faith to work. At salvation, we received faith. Now, it's time to release it. What happens when we speak forth the Word and put it into action? Our faith goes to work and brings Earth into a collision course with the will of Heaven.

At the day's end, I want to be someone who speaks forth words of faith. When people ask, "Larry, are you one of those *faith* people?" I want to proudly affirm, "Yes! What would you rather have me be – one of the *doubt* people?" I don't deny circumstances. I don't pretend away problems. Rather, I want to commit to say what God is saying.

As we do this, new realities are created. Hopeless situations turn around. Mountains bow. Demons flee. What's the end result? God's glory covering the Earth. This is your litmus test to evaluating whether you are dealing with the counterfeit or genuine. The counterfeit is all about stuff. Material wealth. Promotion. Such are not inherently bad things, but they are not the end goals of Christianity. May the end result of our faith confessions be God's glory covering the Earth as water covers the sea. The word of God released from your mouth is a spiritual sword that demolishes the powers of darkness and unleashes the Kingdom of God.

POINT OF BREAKTHROUGH

I have included a section at the end of each chapter providing a summary of the main topic that we explored.

RECOMMENDED READING

In addition, I will be providing lists of highly recommended resources for further study. These authors will take you into greater depths of understanding and revelation on some of the topics that we reviewed in part.

FOR MORE...

Go to www.mybreakthroughfaith.com for more dynamic resources on each of these topics.

Part One

~~

UNDERSTANDING BREAKTHROUGH FAITH

1

UNWRAP YOUR GIFT

~~

*For it is by grace you have been saved, through
faith—and this is not from yourselves, it is
the gift of God.* —EPHESIANS 2:8 NIV

This faith to move mountains and supernaturally transform every
impossible situation that comes against us is not out of our reach. It's
not some upgraded version of faith reserved for the spiritually elite. Are
you a Christian? If so, then this means you have *already received* breakthrough faith. It was God's gift to you, to both save you eternally and
empower you to live victoriously while upon the earth.[1]

If we are believers in Christ, it is not necessary for us to run around,
trying to get faith as if it's something we don't already possess. Rather,
it is more like unwrapping a gift that we have already received. At the
moment of our salvation, we received the key that transforms hope into
reality, possibilities into solutions, and God's Word into life-changing
supernatural power. And that key is faith. It's one of the most frequently
preached about and written about topics in Christianity today—but do
we really understand what faith is and how to use it to walk out a lifestyle of supernatural breakthrough?

I want to help you be aware of what you have already received at the moment of salvation and show you how to put it to work in your everyday life. The faith you received is not wimpy. It's not watered down. It's not some junior faith that is in need of a constant upgrade. You received supernatural faith from a supernatural God the moment you were born again.

Together we will navigate through some false understandings and ideas about faith, press through the deceptions, and then learn how to put the truth into action. Throughout the book I will share my up-and-down story with understanding and activating faith, as I experienced *extremes* on both ends of the spectrum. Now, by God's grace, I am moving toward a healthy, Bible-based balance of what faith looks like and how it functions. My vision is to stir up the breakthrough faith inside each of you—faith that perseveres through every obstacle and obtains the promises of God.

Throughout this journey together, we will establish solid, Scripture-based foundations on what faith is and how to put it to work in our lives. This is why the book is broken up into two sections: Understanding Faith and Activating Faith. Many books about faith focus on one or the other, but I believe that in order to activate faith we need to have a solid, biblical understanding of what it actually is, where it comes from, and what it does. For faith principles to work effectively, they must be built on the pillar of the knowledge of God. Otherwise, at the first sign of resistance, we will break.

At the moment of our salvation, we received the key that transforms hope into reality, possibilities into solutions, and God's Word into life-changing supernatural power.

There are three groups of believers that my book is written for: the first group consists of those who have been striving to diligently work all of the faith principles, but after days, weeks, and even years of confessing, declaring, rebuking, reading, listening, and praying, they feel burned out and spiritually bankrupt. Hold on tight, friend. I believe the Holy Spirit is going to bring you some much-needed encouragement and balance.

The second group is those who need to learn about certain scriptural realities that they have never been exposed to before. In order for them to experience breakthrough, they need to be introduced to some new, and perhaps unusual, ways that God moves. To many, these realities include supernatural healing, deliverance, freedom from oppression, and restoration—to name just a few of the more popular topics. I am so excited to share these keys with you, keys that are going to birth within you a hunger to experience God's power in fresh, new, Bible-based ways.

The third group consists of those who are just hungry to experience *more* in their relationship with God. They are not content with a miracle on Sunday and a meltdown on Monday; they are pressing into a lifestyle of sustained, supernatural breakthrough. This desire burns in their hearts (and it should burn in the heart of every believer, for we were made for it). Christianity, in its current shape and form, does not satisfy them. There is a resounding cry from deep inside their spirit, telling them that there is a "new normal" available.

Two Types of Faith

There are two types of faith believers tend to gravitate toward. First, we can fall prey to *experiential faith*. This is a counterfeit understanding of faith that is built on personal experience, not the eternal, unchanging truth of Scripture. An example of this type of faith is that because we are sick and showing no signs of improvement, experiential faith begins to assume that God's overall will is sickness for our lives. Or another example is that we believe that God does not want to restore a hurting marriage because we see many examples of other people in our lives who ended up getting divorced, even though they prayed for reconciliation.

Experiential faith emerges if we are going through something—a sickness, family problem, addiction, trial, or bondage—and rather than stand on what God's eternal Word says and agree with the solutions presented in Scripture, we start to use our circumstances to define who

God is for us. If we don't experience immediate healing, then we start to believe that He is *not* the healer. If restoration in a relationship does not take place overnight, we begin to think that He might *not* be a restorer. This perspective shapes how we end up praying about our problems. Bad reports. Hopeless situations. Impossibilities.

Experiential faith often appears to be the most popular and damaging perspective for us to adopt when it comes to faith. We cannot treat God's character like it changes every time we go through a difficult season or situation. He does not respond one day, only to be silent on the next. He does not reveal His nature as healer, deliverer, or restorer on Sunday, only to completely change His character on Monday. Experiential faith is *not* faith at all; it is a counterfeit and denies the constancy of God's eternal nature. It is in direct opposition to what Scripture tells us about the Lord Jesus Christ, who *"is the same yesterday and today and forever"* (Heb. 13:8 NIV).

Does God use our suffering and sickness for His ultimate glory? Absolutely and thoroughly, as He is a God who refuses to let anything be wasted. The key, however, is being able to appropriately identify *where* our circumstances come from and refusing to let them adjust the way we see God.

The second type of faith—and this is what I am pursuing at all costs and the lifestyle Jesus is inviting all of us into—is the lifestyle of *breakthrough faith.* And I have some incredible news for you: this is your inheritance as a believer in the Lord Jesus Christ! Gone is the ridiculous idea that "You don't have enough faith to…" and you name the Scripture-based breakthrough you are believing for. The revelation of breakthrough faith completely destroys the concept of "levels of faith," for every person who has given his or her life to the Lord Jesus Christ has received breakthrough faith. The time has come to learn how to activate it and walk in it as your everyday Christian experience.

THE CEILING

The entire essence of this teaching is based on an account in Mark 2 that I have come to affectionately call "Faith that Breaks through the Ceiling." The ceiling is whatever stands between you and the promises that God's Word legally authorizes you to possess. Examples of these ceilings include the disappointment of perceived unanswered prayers, circumstances that did not work out, or those downright overwhelming seasons where the phrase "hell on earth" takes on new, personal meaning for us.

Faith does not accept any ceiling or any boundary that prevents us from experiencing God's promises coming to pass in our lives. This is the attitude we will be developing in the pages ahead—one that holds on tight to what God has said in His Word, and refuses to let go until what He said becomes what we experience.

We have become inundated with teaching on faith. Many of us are overwhelmed with Kingdom principles—the how-tos of faith. But when it comes down to the foundational level, many believers are not truly grounded in what they believe about who God is, what the Scripture says, and the supernatural lifestyle Jesus modeled for us to live. As a result, we become susceptible to embracing the experiential faith that changes every time we face opposition.

We may persevere for a season, but ultimately, when things get to be too overwhelming, we throw in the towel, adjust our theology, and conclude that God might not be interested in getting us through our situation or circumstance. That whole business of transforming impossible situations and bringing Heaven to earth sounds more like pie-in-the-sky ideology than the normal Christian life. This should not be the case at all. I am going to help you activate a faith that can break through any situation, season, or circumstance.

RESTORING BREAKTHROUGH FAITH

We have been given this tool of faith to release Heaven's solution into every situation that does not line up with God's perfect will for our lives. Heaven contains every solution that will transform the circumstances and challenges we face on earth. The lack we experience is not on God's end. He has everything that we need to enjoy victory in this lifetime. The lack exists on earth because there is a disagreement between two worlds and two different realities. God's will and agenda for created order was completely good and *never* involved a separation between Heaven and earth. Sin created this gulf. But the blood of Jesus made it possible for these two worlds to be reconnected once again. Jesus would have never given us the Lord's Prayer as a model if He was not interested in bringing two worlds together: on earth as it is in Heaven (see Matt. 6:10).

When something on earth is in disagreement with the culture and climate of Heaven, it should not be okay with us. In fact, it is completely unacceptable. Paul identifies us as ambassadors of the Lord Jesus Christ (see 2 Cor. 5:20), representing the culture of heaven while on earth. Before we are citizens of a country, governmental system, or even the planet earth, our citizenship is first in Heaven (see Phil. 3:20). This citizenship has everything to do with the ultimate purpose of faith, for Christianity is all about bringing Heaven to earth.

The early disciples and followers of Christ recognized this. Every time faith in Christ was demonstrated and released miracles, signs, wonders, and healings, Heaven's culture was being established on earth. Everything that was normal in God's world was coming into this one. This is our primary mission while living on this planet, according to the Lord's Prayer.

I place no restrictions on how much of Heaven is available for here and now. We leave that up to God. In the meantime, we are called to embrace this commission with great joy, knowing that through faith we get to participate in bringing divine alignment between God's solutions and our impossibilities.

Prolific author and prophet Kris Vallotton makes the following comment about the early followers of Christ and their overall mission:

> Apostles are not only sent; they are sent for a very specific purpose. The word "apostle" comes from the secular Roman world. The Romans were very aggressive about expanding their empire. They wisely employed the strategy of Alexander the Great, who established the Greek Empire by conquering kingdoms and then culturizing them in Greek ways.[2]

They were not just disciples—ones who learned from the Master. They were apostles—sent ones, called to culturize planet earth with the ways and culture of Heaven. This is our mission too! Faith is not only about getting us into Heaven one day, but following the apostles' lead and making our world look as much like Heaven as possible. As ambassadors and emissaries of Christ, Heaven is our place of citizenship, not just an eternal resting place. Heaven can have influence and impact *now*, on earth, in our sphere of influence, through our faith!

WE ARE EQUIPPED FOR THE TASK

In the pages ahead, we are going to go on a journey together. Whatever you currently think about faith, I ask that you keep an open mind and let the Holy Spirit come and lead you into all truth. My heart burns to see the body of Christ unlock the power of breakthrough faith and bring the supernatural power of Heaven to earth—in our lives and in our world. I want each of us to walk in sustained, consistent victory over the unbiblical circumstances that come against us. These things are not God's sovereign plan or purpose for our lives.

Faith is not only about getting us into Heaven one day, but following the apostles' lead and making our world look as much like Heaven as possible.

If you are currently dealing with circumstances that are not in line with God's Word—either in your life or someone else's—I want to equip you with practical tools to break through every obstacle, press through every circumstance, and experience victory in every season of your life, in Jesus' name!

POINT OF BREAKTHROUGH

We already received breakthrough faith at the moment of our salvation; the key is understanding what we already possess and activating it in order to live a lifestyle of sustained victory!

IDENTIFY THE GREAT DECEPTION

~~

And when they could not come near Him because of
the crowd, they uncovered the roof where He was.
So when they had broken through, they let down the
bed on which the paralytic was lying. —MARK 2:4

What is the *great deception* I am referring to here? It is simply this: *everything that happens in life is God's will.* It says that, "Whatever I experience in life, whether good or bad, is God's divine orchestration and come directly from His hand." If God wanted us to "take life" lying down, embracing everything that happened to us as His sovereign plan, then He would not have invited us to walk in a supernatural lifestyle of breakthrough faith.

The four men in Mark 2 brought their paralyzed friend to the house where Jesus was teaching. It was so full of people that they could not get in. They could have seen this opposition as God's sovereign will not to heal their friend. But the problem was that they had already heard too much about Jesus' miracles and power. They heard about what He did for *everyone* who came to Him, and the testimony they heard about Jesus actually revealed who Jesus was. He was compassionate. He was the Healer. His identity was unchanging, and these men knew that if they got their paralyzed friend into the Presence of the Healer, his situation would be transformed. They had such strong faith in this Jesus, who miraculously transformed circumstances, that they literally broke through a ceiling and lowered their friend down, right in front of Jesus. Oh, how Jesus loves breakthrough faith!

The "God is in control" approach to everything we go through is a great deception that completely discounts the reality of our enemy, demolishes any opportunity to exercise faith, and dangerously skews the very nature, character, and activity of God. God is truly sovereign, but when it comes to Him manipulating and controlling certain things that take place on planet earth, we must be aware that there are enemy forces at work too.

When we start attributing things to God that are not His doing, but are instead the result of sin, or, even worse, the direct assault of our enemy, satan, we begin to introduce uncertainty into our relationship with Him because we see His character incorrectly. It's skewed. We try to soothe ourselves by packaging it in silly theological language like, "God has a purpose" or "God has a plan" or "God is good," but deep down, we end up with a pile of unanswered questions that were never designed to go unanswered.

This is not to say that there is no mystery to God and that absolutely everything that happens in life will make total sense. It won't. However, there are some very clear and defined realities we need to settle in our hearts concerning God—who He is, what He's like, and what He does and does not do, if we are to relate to Him properly. In this section, we will begin to identify the true source of pain, torment, and affliction in our lives.

2

RECOGNIZE THE BATTLE

~~

Lest satan should take advantage of us; for we are
not ignorant of his devices. —2 CORINTHIANS 2:11

W e have an enemy. He is not some theological concept. He is more
than just bad thoughts and temptations. The devil, satan, is our
adversary and antagonist. I don't say this with intention to frighten but
rather with a purpose to educate. In view of the enemy's reality and
agenda, it is absolutely ridiculous for us to identify *everything* that happens to us as God's sovereign will and perfect plan.

Let me illustrate. Even though the Bible told me there was a real
devil and real demons, experientially this did not become an up-close-
and-personal reality for me until January of 2012. I was at a revival
service in Orlando, Florida. Toward the end of the meeting, as the
worship team was passionately exalting Jesus and the crowds were experiencing wave after wave of God's glorious Presence, I started walking
around the sanctuary praying. As I briefly looked down, I saw a small
group of people gathered around a girl. She looked like she was in her
twenties. Her eyes were black, her face was contorted, and she was biting
herself. Blood was tricking down her arm.

I was amazed at the honor the small group was showing her. They didn't push her up to the platform for some type of public spectacle or highly charged exorcism scenario. In fact, I recall a woman cradling the demonized girl in her arms while the others were quietly praying over her. Out of respect for what God was doing, I moved on quickly as to not dishonor the young woman who was being set free from demonic torment. And praise God, by the time I ran into her and the group later on, she was in her right mind, appearing completely free.

God's perfect will was not for that young woman to be in torment and bondage to some demonic, oppressive spirit. His will happened on the *other side* of that small group of people praying for her, honoring her, loving her, and declaring the Word of God and the power of Jesus' name over her. This was done in faith so that the Spirit of God could set her free. And He did!

BREAKING OUR AGREEMENT WITH DARKNESS AND WISING UP

Faith is the supernatural force that breaks agreement with the enemy and releases the solutions of Heaven into our circumstances. Again, we see the true nature of faith at work as the power and resources of God's world flow into ours, overriding what the enemy intends for our destruction. When we bow to the enemy's deceptions, we are agreeing with darkness and thereby giving him an open door into our lives.

One of the main ways we agree with darkness is by attributing the work of the enemy to the sovereign will of God. As long as we believe God is causing the destructive, negative, afflicting circumstances in our lives—realities that the Bible clearly attributes to the work of darkness—the longer we will remain in bondage to deception. Instead of combating circumstances in faith, we will simply yield to them, believing they are God's doing.

Christians should refuse to get trampled on by the enemy and fight back from a position of victory. When we allow the devil to wreak havoc in our lives, it is not because we are dealing with a worthy opponent; it is because we are actually giving the devil the only power he has available—our agreement.

> **Faith is the supernatural force that breaks agreement with the enemy and releases the solutions of Heaven into our circumstances.**

Before we explore the foundations of faith, discover what it means to persevere in faith, and position ourselves to receive breakthrough by faith, we need to understand the contrary forces that have been working against the people of God since day one. Do you know what the enemy's great deception is? It is nothing less than creating ignorance of his involvement in the world. Dr. Jack Graham notes, "That's a central goal of satan's, to make Christians doubt his existence, his power, his prowess in causing destruction in our lives."[3] If the devil's not involved, then everything bad must logically come from the hand of God.

ACKNOWLEDGING OUR ENEMY

God does not want us to be ignorant of the devil's sly devices. The serpent of old would love to convince the world that he is some non-existent, fictitious, fairy tale figure, that he is the making of Hollywood. Countless Christians actually deny the realities of hell, demons, and a literal devil altogether. The fruit of this deception is absolutely startling because if we do not believe in the contrary forces of darkness, all of the evil and opposition in life ultimately come from the hand of God. We must acknowledge the reality of the devil and his dominion of darkness if we want to experience breakthrough.

This does not make it legal for us to become overly preoccupied with darkness. My pastor always says that there are ditches on both sides of the road—and both of them are bad and should be avoided at all costs. Unholy preoccupation with darkness is the other ditch the enemy would love us to fall into, where we spend all of our time running after demons, duking it out with the devil, rebuking, renouncing, and delivering—spending so much time on the defense that nothing offensive takes place. Darkness gains ground when it keeps the church living on the defense, but it trembles when a people rise up and recognize the apostolic potential of their faith.

MOVING FROM DEFENSE TO OFFENSE

The devil does not tremble at those who are fighting him all of the time. If we are spending most of our Christian lives fighting with the devil, this means we believe some major lies about him. He is defeated and we are victorious! To fight the devil is to fight one who has already been defeated, disarmed, stripped of his power and completely overthrown. A.W. Tozer describes it this way: "I'm not afraid of the devil. The devil can handle me—he's got judo I never heard of. But he can't handle the One to whom I'm joined; he can't handle the One to whom I'm united; he can't handle the One whose nature dwells in my nature."[4] The devil is not frightened of ignorant believers; however, he is absolutely terrified of those who recognize and represent the Victorious One who lives on the inside of them.

The whole of hell trembles at the believer who recognizes his or her inheritance, and lives in an offensive posture toward darkness. Again, this does not involve making darkness a focal point. Rather, the knowledge of the Holy One is what feeds and fuels the victorious Christian. The person who makes God his or her main focus, pursuit, and conquest is the very one who will carry Heaven's solutions into every arena of life. When God Himself becomes the glorious quest of the church, darkness will become subdued in an unprecedented manner.

It's time to transition from the defensive to the offensive. Author Francis Frangipane says, "The Spirit of God does not want us to merely tolerate oppression; He desires us to conquer it."[5] This is what putting breakthrough faith into action looks like. Faith is not just about holding down the fort and fighting off the enemy; it is about gaining new ground for God's Kingdom. By studying the Word of God together, I want to help you gain new territory in your life!

POINT OF BREAKTHROUGH

Not everything that happens in our lives is the sovereign will and plan of God. We must recognize the influence of the devil—who is our enemy and adversary—in order to exercise breakthrough faith in every situation we face.

~~~

RECOMMENDED READING

Unseen by Dr. Jack Graham

Happy Intercessor by Beni Johnson

Spirit Wars by Kris Vallotton

This Day We Fight by Francis Frangipane

3

IDENTIFY YOUR ENEMY

~~

The first step on the way to victory is to
recognize the enemy. —CORRIE TEN BOOM[6]

We are in a battle *against* a real enemy. He is real and he is the antagonist of every single believer. He is not some figment of Christianity's collective imagination or some guy running around in a red suit with a pitchfork and an arrow-shaped tail. We must recognize the enemy's reality if we are to experience the victory God has ordained for us. Otherwise, we will continue to fall right into the devil's trap and attribute all of his works of darkness to the sovereign hand of God.

In this chapter I want to teach you how to become aware of your enemy without becoming grossly preoccupied with him. Pretending the devil away keeps us believing that God is responsible for all of the problems and circumstances we face, while focusing on the devil too much distracts us from a Christianity of conquest and prevents forward momentum. It makes perfect sense then that the enemy would like nothing more than for us to either make a big deal out of him, believing he is stronger than God, or believe that he does not exist. Both of these thoughts are lies, and that is all the serpent can ever do—lie. C.S. Lewis put it best in his classic book *The Screwtape Letters*:

There are two equal and opposite errors into which our race can fall about the devils. One is to disbelieve in their existence. The other is to believe, and to feel an excessive and unhealthy interest in them. They themselves are equally pleased by both errors and hail a materialist or a magician with the same delight.[7]

By entertaining either one of these deceptions, the devil gets what he wants: Christians filled with power who believe they are powerless against the circumstances they encounter. Either God is responsible for all of the bad stuff or the devil is this overwhelming, super-strong adversary we will spend our entire lives battling against, and always losing. In the last chapter we discussed the danger of neglecting the truth of our enemy, but we can also overemphasize him too.

DON'T GIVE THE DEVIL TOO MUCH CREDIT

I don't want us to invest too much emphasis on the devil here. He's simply not worth our time. However, we need to be informed about who we are dealing with if we are going to approach faith the right way. Many believers out there hold to an orthodox view of Scripture and believe in the reality of the devil and demons. However, they fail to recognize the devil's active involvement in humanity and they don't really grasp the enemy's sinister agenda against every single person on the planet. We need to study the following topic with balance and wisdom in order to walk in the victory that breakthrough faith releases.

As a middle schooler, I was intrigued by horror movies, particularly the supernatural ones—*The Omen, The Exorcist, Rosemary's Baby*, etc. In the last decade, the only thing that has changed are the titles and increasingly graphic nature of gore, sexuality, and darkness present on the movie screen. A generation is still being enticed by the works of darkness. Why is this?

This is because there appears to be power available in the darkness. Once again, the devil is assuming his place as the author of lies, because the only power he has is what we give him. When the prince of darkness is the front and center of our focus, he becomes powerful. He becomes a formidable foe, not because he actually is, but because of our emphasis and focus upon him. The devil only gets scary when we believe that he is. The reality is our enemy is a defeated foe, crushed under the feet of King Jesus. This is why he uses media, television, and Hollywood to try and convince the world, and yes, even deceive believers into thinking he is more frightening and powerful than he really is. This is simply not the case. When it comes to exercising breakthrough faith, if we are under the assumption that the devil is a force to be reckoned with, we are going to live in defense mode rather than on the offense.

> **Pretending the devil away keeps us believing that God is responsible for all of the problems and circumstances we face, while focusing on the devil too much distracts us from a Christianity of conquest and prevents forward momentum.**

Preachers, teachers, evangelists, and anyone involved in ministry can easily fall prey to this overemphasis of the devil as well. We just make it sound more spiritual than watching horror movies—but I believe it is as equally dangerous! Perry Stone gives a fantastic illustration in his book *Exposing Satan's Playbook*, where his mother actually tried to run a spiritual intervention for him. She went to a key leader in the ministry and expressed her concerns about Perry, noting that since he became obsessed with studying the demonic, all sorts of unusual phenomena had plagued him. Horrible things started happening, including actual "visible manifestations of spirits cloaked in dark garments and hoods hiding their faces."[8]

The devil does whatever he can to draw us into his world of darkness through intrigue. Perry Stone shares the exceptional advice that this ministry leader gave him: "As long as you concentrate on demons, they will show up. If you preach and concentrate on Jesus, then He will show up."[9] That statement makes me want to shout!

So Perry made a shift in his emphasis, from darkness to light, from focusing on the devil to keeping Jesus at the center of all things. He concluded that as a result of the shift in focus, "the presence of Christ began to manifest and deliver individuals from the oppression of the enemy."[10] Interestingly enough, overemphasis on the devil and his demons does not bring deliverance to those in torment and captivity. When we give the enemy more attention than he is due, we end up exaggerating his power. This actually keeps people in bondage and torment, rather than introducing these individuals to the author of freedom, hope, and healing—Jesus Christ.

> **Our enemy is a defeated foe, crushed under the feet of King Jesus.**

After learning this valuable lesson, Perry Stone gives us a powerful key to activating our breakthrough faith and releasing the supernatural power of God: we are to shift focus from the defeated one who deceives with trickery and illusions, and exalt the Greater One living inside of us, who has all authority, all power, and all dominion. Darkness does not stand a chance in the Presence of King Jesus!

BASIC FACTS ABOUT OUR ENEMY

With all of this in mind, there are some basic facts we need to keep in mind concerning the adversary if we want to begin living a lifestyle of breakthrough faith. Peter reminds us, *"Be sober, be vigilant; because your adversary the devil walks about like a roaring lion, seeking whom he may devour"* (1 Pet. 5:8).

The Enemy Is Our Adversary

The devil is not God's adversary, as God already defeated him at the cross of Calvary. Rather, he is *our* adversary. The Amplified Bible emphasizes this, with Peter writing *"for that enemy of yours, the devil..."* The very name *satan*, in Hebrew, means "adversary."[11] His tactics are not aimed at God; they are rather directed toward us. After all, God is not going to believe the devil's lies; the only people capable of believing his deceptions and thereby granting him an inroad into their lives are human beings, like you and me. This is not intended to scare any of us; it is only meant to simply raise awareness that our adversary is not God but the devil.

The Enemy Is a Devourer

God is not the One who devours and destroys—this job description belongs to the devil. It is vital that we classify anything that threatens to destroy life or assault the promises of God as devilish in origin.

The Enemy Devours Those Who Allow Him

There is a secret in this passage that arms us for victory. Unfortunately, it gets lost amidst us focusing on the devil, his evil schemes, and his being like a lion (he is *not* a lion; he only masquerades as one). Peter tells us that the devil is *"seeking whom he may devour,"* with the key word being *may*. In this book, I am going to arm you to stare the devil's tactics in the face and with burning words of faith declare, "No, you *may* not!" I want us to stop giving him permission to devour our lives.

The Enemy Is Our Foe and Antagonist

Ephesians 6 reminds us that we are in a battle. Paul writes,

> *Put on the whole armor of God, that you may be able to stand against the wiles of the devil. For we do not wrestle against flesh and blood, but against principalities, against powers, against the rulers of the darkness of this age, against spiritual hosts of wickedness in the heavenly places* (Ephesians 6:11-12).

The devil is defeated, but nevertheless he is looking for an inroad of agreement because he is well aware of the destruction he can bring to lives that say yes to his deceptions. Paul reminds us to be on guard—not against our Father God who is out to get us, but rather against the strategies of the devil, the *evil one* (see Matt. 6:13; John 17:15; 2 Thess. 3:3). You may chuckle at that, but we seriously need a paradigm adjustment if we are going to walk in supernatural, breakthrough faith. The devil is our enemy, not our Father. God is not fighting against us; He is fighting *for* us, equipping us with every resource necessary to stand victorious in the day of battle (see Rom. 8:31)! The fight is fixed and the battle is already won.

The Enemy Is No Respecter of Innocence

This is obvious in a world stained by child abuse, sex trafficking, and the unspeakable atrocities committed against the innocent. It is easy to let these realities cause us to desire a speedy return of Christ. The reality is that while we are still occupying planet earth, we must recognize that these abominations are the by-products of a devil who is deceiving people left and right. He is obtaining an inroad into their lives, gaining a foothold, developing a stronghold, and ultimately achieving a stranglehold. Again, we must acknowledge the horrors in this world as the devil's architecture, otherwise we begin to distort and pervert the good character of God.

The Enemy Is Our Accuser

John writes in the Book of Revelation that the devil, who is *"the accuser of our brethren, who accused them before our God day and night, has been cast down"* (Rev. 12:10). This Scripture reveals that the devil no longer accuses us before God; rather, he accuses us directly.

Do you know why he is unable to accuse us before God, bringing up our sin, our works, our issues, and our unworthiness before the throne of Heaven? It is because he knows that God would have one eternal response to every single one of his accusations: the blood of Jesus was enough. In the Book of Job we see the devil presenting Job before God (see Job 1:6-12), but I do not believe that such a scenario is possible under the New Covenant. While the enemy cannot accuse us before God, he can accuse us directly and try to deceive us out of believing that the blood of Jesus is enough to make us acceptable in God's sight (see Hebrews 3:13). I believe this is the chief revelation that he will try to challenge in our lives, for it is Jesus' blood and our testimony that ultimately spell defeat for him.

> **God is not fighting against us; He is fighting *for* us, equipping us with every resource necessary to stand victorious in the day of battle.**

POINT OF BREAKTHROUGH

We recognize the enemy's tactics, not to become overly preoccupied with darkness, but to predict his moves and thwart his advances in our lives.

~~

RECOMMENDED READING

The Screwtape Letters by C.S. Lewis

Exposing Satan's Playbook by Perry Stone

Eight Ways to Keep the Devil Under Your Feet by Joyce Meyer

4

LIVE FROM THE POSITION OF VICTORY

~~

And they overcame him by the blood of the Lamb and
by the word of their testimony. —REVELATION 12:11

This chapter is dedicated to arming you with the truth about the ene-my's current defeated position. These realities must be our anchors because if satan can convince us otherwise, he has got us right where he wants us. Believers are not typically defeated because satan comes in and overpowers them; they are defeated because they come into agreement with him and *willingly* believe his lies.

We are aware of the devil so we can effectively resist him. Rest assured, he will come against us and try to accuse us for one thing or another. Maybe we sinned. Maybe we have something in our past that brings shame or guilt. Maybe we have been in a season of running from God and the devil wants to convince us that God is through with us—that we're damaged goods. Maybe we are dealing with sick-ness, torment, or some form of major trial in our lives, and he wants to convince us that it is our fault or our sin that brought us to this place of torment.

We shut the accuser's mouth every time we declare the eternal power of Jesus' blood! It did not simply cover our sins and mistakes; it totally abolished them and blotted them out of existence (see Acts 3:19). The blood of Jesus makes us accusation-free before the eyes of a Holy God. Testify of the power of Jesus' blood and, in particular, declare how that precious blood saved you!

The enemy's ultimate goal is to try and thwart God's ministry of reconciliation and restoration in the earth. He is fighting a losing battle though. His fate is already sealed and God will get what He desires. In the meantime, this defeated foe is absolutely terrified of us and the unique expression of God's Kingdom we bring to the earth. Yes, each one of us matters! Each of us has tremendous significance. We are significant because of who we carry—the Holy Spirit of God. God Himself lives within us, and that makes us the most powerful threat to darkness the enemy could possibly fathom. Now multiply that threat by the millions of Spirit-filled believers inhabiting the planet, and hell has really got a problem on its hands.

THE ENEMY'S MAIN AGENDA

If the enemy can keep us convinced that God is actually the One who steals, kills, and destroys, we will continue to live out a powerless form of Christianity where being robbed, slaughtered, and defeated is the norm. A.W. Tozer actually defines this as unbelief—"attributing to God the character of Satan."[12] To believe incorrectly about God is actually likened to unbelief. As a result, we will not place our faith in the One we believe is against us. We will not use faith to confront and overcome our problems because we believe that the problems coming against us are God's sovereign will. By praying against them, we believe that we are warring against God. God uses problems. God teaches through circumstances. I refuse to deny those realities and promote some ridiculous happy-go-lucky gospel. With that said, even though God can use adverse circumstances and use negative situations for His glory, He is not their author.

> **The blood of Jesus makes us accusation-free before the eyes of the Holy God.**

Neil T. Anderson, author of *The Bondage Breaker*, observes that the "major strategy of Satan is to distort the character of God and the truth of who we are. He can't change God and he can't do anything to change our identity and position in Christ. If, however, he can get us to believe a lie, we will live as though our identity in Christ isn't true."[13] It is so important that we build a solid faith foundation if we are going to experience a lifestyle of victory, and this all starts with being grounded in who God is, and, in turn, knowing who we are in Him.

EVALUATE THE FRUIT OF YOUR CIRCUMSTANCES

How do we know if what we are experiencing is from God or from the enemy? Here is a surefire biblical litmus test. Jesus said, *"The thief does not come except to steal, and to kill, and to destroy. I have come that they may have life, and that they may have it more abundantly"* (John 10:10). Think of it this way for a moment: if the circumstance or situation we are currently dealing with steals, kills, or destroys, there is a strong likelihood that we are dealing with the devil (we are definitely not dealing with God). If our situation steals time, emotion, joy, opportunity, health, finances, rest, mental stability, and every other grace and blessing from the Lord, then it is the thief's handiwork and must be combated.

Perhaps we let him in through a sinful decision we have made. Maybe he's coming against us to see how much agreement he can get from our end. Listen, if we opened a door to the enemy, we can close it at any time we want. The only thing that prevents us from closing doors to the devil is continuing to believe his lies. If we have sinned, then we should simply repent. Jesus' blood has made us completely clean! The devil wants us to wallow in any state of mind that will maintain agreement with his deceptive activity in our lives.

No matter how the process of theft, murder, or destruction began in our lives, know this: the devil wants it to continue. Here is the good news: you can put an end to it. This is the power of breakthrough faith. It arms us with the resolve to say "enough is enough" to every scheme and strategy of the enemy. If we think God is behind the stealing, killing, and destroying, then we will not be inclined to activate faith for victory. This is because we believe we are warring against the "overall good and sovereign plan of God." This is not so. The good plan of God is to see His Kingdom come and His will done in our lives as it is in Heaven.

> **If we opened a door to the enemy,**
> **we can close it at any time.**

TWO ESSENTIAL KEYS TO WALKING IN VICTORY

The Enemy Is Not God's Opposite

The first key to walking in victory over the enemy is recognizing that he is a created being and each of us in Christ has authority over him. He is not eternal. He is in no way, shape, or form "on par" with God. Consider his origins for a moment:

> *You were in Eden, the garden of God; every precious stone*
> *was your covering: the sardius, topaz, and diamond, beryl,*
> *onyx, and jasper, sapphire, turquoise, and emerald with gold.*
> *The workmanship of your timbrels and pipes was prepared*
> *for you on the day you were created* (Ezekiel 28:13).

Pastor Bill Johnson makes a profound statement concerning the devil's identity in his book *Hosting the Presence*: "Never at any time has satan been a threat to God. God is ultimate in power and might, beauty and glory. He is eternal with unlimited measures of all that is good. He is uncreated—has always existed. Satan is limited in every way. God gave him his gifts and abilities at his own creation. There has never been a battle between God and satan."[14]

The devil is not the opposite of God; he is a created being who, if anything, is the opposite of Michael the Archangel.[15] If only Adam and Eve had recognized the full expanse of the dominion they received in Genesis 1. Do you remember what God told them? He gave them dominion over everything that creeps on the earth (see Gen. 1:30). Where was the devil in the beginning? He was creeping on the earth. Man had authority over the serpent, as the serpent was a created, creeping thing. He still is, and because of the cross, this authority has been restored to us!

The Enemy Has Been Defeated, Stripped of Power, and Humiliated

The second key to walking in victory over the enemy is in understanding that we deal with a powerless adversary. Paul wrote,

> [God] disarmed the principalities and powers that were ranged against us and made a bold display and public example of them, in triumphing over them in Him and in it [the cross] (Colossians 2:15 AMP).

When it comes to understanding the devil's place in a believer's life, Colossians 2:15 sums it all up: the enemy is crushed beneath the cross of Calvary. These verses make me think of the timeless hymn penned by the great reformer, Martin Luther. He wrote,

> And though this world, with devils filled, should threaten to undo us,
>
> We will not fear, for God hath willed His truth to triumph through us:
>
> The Prince of Darkness grim, we tremble not for him;
>
> His rage we can endure, for lo, his doom is sure,
>
> One little word shall fell him.[16]

That one little word is revealed in Mark 16:17: *"In My name they will cast out demons."* That beautiful name—the matchless name of Jesus—reminds the enemy time and time again of what took place on Calvary, the eternal victory that was achieved over darkness, and what continues to take place day after day as *"the manifold wisdom of God might be made known by the church to the principalities and powers in the heavenly places"* (Eph. 3:10). The church continues to enforce the victory of Calvary as it serves as God's divine vessel of dispelling darkness throughout the planet. And guess what—you and I are partakers in this victory! Before it is a building or institution, the church is our identity.

To Sum It Up

Not everything that comes our way is God's sovereign will for our life. I pray that the last few chapters have made this abundantly clear. We are in a battle. Were this not so, the armor of God described in Ephesians 6 would not have been listed in the pages of Scripture for us to equip ourselves with. However, we are in a very unusual war. The battle has already been won and the enemy has been defeated. We are not fighting a powerful devil; we are warring from a place of secured, assured victory to enforce what the Bible promises to manifest in our lives and in our world. We are not fighting with God either, trying to convince and connive Him to do what He said He would do. The One who promised is faithful (see Heb. 10:23).

Instead, we are warring against the enemy's deception that works overtime to keep humanity from stepping into God's divine purposes. Faith is the currency to bringing God's divine purposes to pass on the earth. The key to activating this breakthrough faith is not through learning some principle or formula—the devil is not warring against principles, he is not threatened by sermons, teachings, conferences, or ten easy steps. What causes darkness to tremble is a people who realize who their God is, recognize what He has given to them through their inheritance, and who are willing to represent His will accurately. When we use faith based on the character and nature of God, *everything* we ask for will come to pass because we are asking for the desires that are in alignment with who God is. Such faith will not go amiss!

> **We are not fighting a powerful devil; we are warring from a place of secured, assured victory.**

I love Daniel 11:32, which describes what the knowledge of God is intended to build into the people of God: *"but the people who know their God shall stand firm and take action"* (ESV). When we know who God is and exercise faith in agreement and in alignment with His character, we become supernaturally confident that what we are asking, praying, and decreeing is coming to pass. We stand firm against darkness and impossibility, taking action by activating the breakthrough faith inside of us to experience victory over every scheme of the devil. This is what we will be studying in greater detail in the next section.

POINT OF BREAKTHROUGH

The cross has given us complete victory over the devil; the only ground he can gain in our lives is through deceiving us into believing that stealing, killing, and destroying is the work of God, not the agenda of the evil one.

~~~

RECOMMENDED READING

When Heaven Invades Earth by Bill Johnson

Possessing the Gates of the Enemy by Cindy Jacobs

Worship Warfare by Chuck Pierce

PURSUE THE KNOWLEDGE OF GOD

～～

Therefore I also, after I heard of your faith in
the Lord Jesus and your love for all the saints, do
not cease to give thanks for you, making mention
of you in my prayers: that the God of our Lord
Jesus Christ, the Father of glory, may give to
you the spirit of wisdom and revelation in the
knowledge of Him.—EPHESIANS 1:15-17

Talking about faith is one thing; it is another matter completely to put our faith to work. Working faith protects us from destruction and also empowers us to offensively bring ruin and desolation to the powers of darkness that threaten us, our families, our cities, and our planet. Before we can activate this faith correctly, we must understand who our faith is actually in.

A.W. Tozer commented, "Faith depends upon the *character* of God just as a building rests upon its foundation."[17] Why is the knowledge of God's character so important? It is because our faith will only go as far as our revelation of *who God is.* We will not exercise faith for anything beyond who we believe God to be. Who He is gives us a clear picture of what He will and will not do.

Without knowing who God is, our faith is without a solid foundation. It is through a lifestyle of encounter with God that we discover who He is, what He is like, and what we are scripturally licensed to believe Him for. If we do not know what He is really like, or worse, if we base our faith on lies or false ideas about His nature, we will easily come into agreement with the enemy's agenda to wreak havoc upon our lives. God Himself stated, *"My people are destroyed for lack of knowledge"* (Hos. 4:6).

When God prophetically states that His people are destroyed for a lack of knowledge, He was not referring to a deficit of intellectual information, nor was He saying, "My people are being destroyed because they are not putting correct faith principles into practice." Christianity is not about knowing and applying a list of principles for life enhancement; it is about a dynamic experiential relationship with a Living Person.[18] From out of this relationship everything else flows. The New Living Translation of Hosea 4:6 translates God's words this way: *"My people are being destroyed because they don't know Me."*

Author and prophetic voice Dallas Willard makes a startling statement about the importance of the knowledge of God. He wrote, "Failure to know what God is really like and what His law requires destroys the soul, ruins society, and leaves people to eternal ruin."[19] This is exactly what we will explore in the following chapters.

> **Our faith will only go as far as our revelation of *who God is*.**

I want to help you build your faith upon a solid foundation so you never play into the enemy's hand again, believing his lies, and missing out on God's promises coming to pass in your life. After all, to know God is to love Him, and to love Him is to long to be like Him. When we are walking out a lifestyle of breakthrough faith, we are truly imitating the Father. This is where we will begin.

5

THE POWER OF IMITATING GOD

～～

Therefore be imitators of God as dear children. —EPHESIANS 5:1

Closeness with God produces people who want to be *like* Him. When we come to know God as our Father in a deeper way, we begin to discover who we are as His sons and daughters and what we are able to accomplish through faith. Paul was intentional with the language he used in Ephesians 5:1, connecting the practice of imitating God with our identity as His children.

There is no one closer to us in this life than those who gave birth to us. Yet, there is One who is far closer to us and more deeply acquainted with us than even our earthly parents—*our Father in Heaven*. We are called to draw near to Him as beloved sons and daughters today. We are called to behold Him like never before. In order to imitate God accurately, we must first behold Him clearly, which requires closeness.

As we pursue the knowledge of His character, His nature, and what He is like, we receive a clearer picture of the One we are called to imitate and represent to the world. The degree to which we represent God accurately is entirely wrapped up in our level of intimacy with Him. If we have the religious motions down and know all of the Bible principles to "living a happy life," getting our prayers answered, and looking like a fairly well-adjusted Christian, but have no knowledge of what our God is really like, our imitation will not be accurate. Breakthrough is not sustained. God is not some principle to be plugged into a prayer; He is a Person who invites us into a deep experiential relationship with Himself.

There are two roadblocks that must be removed if we are to enjoy closeness and intimacy with God, and, as a result, reflect Him to the world through a life of sustained victory.

ROADBLOCK #1: RELIGION IS NOT INTIMACY

A key to walking out the supernatural lifestyle with breakthrough faith is aligning ourselves with the desires and heartbeat of God. And to do this, we need to know Him. A.W. Tozer noted, "We can never know who or what we are till we know at least something of what God is."[20] When we know God *as He is*, we will be able to accurately represent Him to the world around us. The ability to represent God requires closeness while religion continues to keep God at a distance. This makes it easy to claim Christianity with our lips and spiritual practices but live in a manner that is ultimately disconnected from God.

The people in Hosea's day behaved much like many in the church world do today. They wanted to receive the fruit of principles without intimate knowledge of the Person of God. They thought if they sang the right songs, prayed the right prayers, and performed the right rituals, Yahweh would allow them to live in their rebellious, sinful state while granting them His blessing and prosperity. Sound familiar?

> *Come, and let us return to the Lord; for He has torn, but He will heal us; He has stricken, but He will bind us up. After two days He will revive us; on the third day He will raise us up, that we may live in His sight. Let us know, let us pursue the knowledge of the Lord. His going forth is established as the morning; He will come to us like the rain, like the latter and former rain to the earth. (Hosea 6:1-3)*

In order to imitate God accurately, we must first behold Him clearly, which requires closeness.

The only problem is that the people who were confessing the correct principles during Hosea's time were completely disconnected from intimate relationship with the Person of Yahweh. It was a mere show they were putting on. They were hoping that by using spiritual-sounding language and religious protocol, they could earn God's good graces.

We are truly experiencing shades of Christianity that reflect the mindset prevalent in the days of Hosea. The people's lips made one declaration, but their hearts were distant from the intimate knowledge of God's nature. The Lord put it this way to the prophet Isaiah: *"Inasmuch as these people draw near with their mouths and honor Me with their lips, but have removed their hearts far from Me..."* (Isa. 29:13).

One common theme we note in the Old Testament Minor Prophets is this: God's people wanted to use God's principles to enhance their lives while living in such a way that was *not* imitating Him. This is the essence of religion and what I see happening in the twenty-first-century church today! We want to apply God's principles for miracles, blessing, and breakthrough apart from drawing near to Him in the place of intimacy. This will not suffice. Here is what Amos said:

> *I can't stand your religious meetings. I'm fed up with your conferences and conventions. I want nothing to do with your religion projects, your pretentious slogans and goals. I'm sick of your fund-raising schemes, your public relations and image making. I've had all I can take of your noisy ego-music. When was the last time you sang to Me?* (Amos 5:21-23 MSG)

God is not against *any* of the things described above—in and of themselves. The problem is that we have exchanged *the most important, precious pursuit* for a thousand lesser things. There are no substitutes to deeply and intimately knowing God. Without Him as the foundation for our lives, all of our religious expressions are worthless and without substance.

Out of God's love and mercy, He will grant blessing and answered prayers for a season to us as we go through the external motions of worship. However, it will not take long to realize that such a lifestyle is not sustainable over any length of time. The Father desires intimacy with us, for it is only out of intimacy that we are able to step into our glorious identity as a people chosen and anointed to represent God on the earth. The supernatural fruit of faith is one way that God is represented and mirrored through His people. This fruit includes a life that sustains power, victory, and breakthrough.

> **There are no substitutes to deeply and intimately knowing God.**

ROADBLOCK #2: INACCURATE REPRESENTATION

The character of God developed within us defines how we pray and steward our faith. Our hunger is for God alone—nothing else. We burn to know Him deeply, for when we know Him we are able to imitate Him. Joyce Meyer says that "we are to have ways and traits like God. His character is to be duplicated in us—His sons and daughters."[21]

The knowledge of God is not an invitation for *more* in quantity— it's not about more Bible reading, more church activities, more prayer, more spiritual stuff, and more works. It simply begins with a posture of the heart that echoes the cry of David in Psalm 27:8: *"When You said, 'Seek My face,' my heart said to You, 'Your face, Lord, I will seek.'"*

The problem is that we live disconnected from our inheritance, which is enjoying closeness with almighty God. Life throws a lot at us. "Busy" is the four-letter word of our day. There is so much going on, from our careers to our education, from our family to maintaining good health, that it is so easy to treat God like the proverbial time clock that we punch once or twice a week. The enemy exploits this big time, as he trembles at the thought of a people who actually realize all they have inherited through the blood of Jesus.

The devil wants us to believe all there is to Christianity is church, religious activities, and principles for life enhancement. By keeping us in this cycle, he prevents us from imitating God and exercising darkness-demolishing breakthrough faith. Even though he tries to use several different boundaries and barriers to keep us from representing God well, the reality is that God made provision in advance to take care of these obstructions.

We can never measure up to and represent the Father accurately in our own strength—and God knew that before He ever created us. The cross was God's divine remedy to every boundary and hindrance that thwarted humanity from knowing Him accurately. The blood of Jesus made us worthy to be inhabited by the Spirit of God. Because of Pentecost, God now empowers us to accurately represent Himself to the world. This is because we are filled with Him. To imitate God is to represent Him, and to represent Him is to activate breakthrough faith! In fact, one of His very names is "Lord of the Breakthrough" (see 2 Sam. 5:20).

POINT OF BREAKTHROUGH

A lifestyle of breakthrough and victory begins with intimately knowing God's character and nature. Our intimacy with God determines how accurately we imitate Him, and our imitation of God determines the level of victory that we sustain in our lives.

~

RECOMMENDED READING

Pursuit of the Holy by Corey Russell

Knowing God Intimately by Joyce Meyer

Secrets to Imitating God by Bill Johnson

6

A PERSON, NOT PRINCIPLES

~~~

No longer do I call you servants, for a servant does not know what his master is doing; but I have called you friends, for all things that I heard from My Father I have made known to you.—JOHN 15:15

Relating to the Person of God is our foundation of faith. By enjoying friendship with Him instead of simply plugging in principles, we position ourselves to walk in greater dimensions of breakthrough, victory, signs, wonders, and miracles than we ever imagined possible. Faith is so much more than a formula that causes us to "get something" out of God.

For years, I attended a church where faith was reduced to principles for life application, personal success, and financial enrichment. For many people who embrace this perspective, the Bible becomes a "vending machine" formula. If we put in the right confession, prayer, or declaration of a Scripture verse, God is obligated to respond by giving us what we asked for. This is a gross perversion of one of the most powerful laws in the universe, and that is the law of decreeing God's Word. The problem was not that all the principles being taught were bad, but rather that the principles were divorced from enjoying closeness and friendship with God.

Hosea captured God's heart concerning this perspective:

*For I desire and delight in dutiful steadfast love and good-
ness, not sacrifice, and the knowledge of and acquaintance
with God more than burnt offerings* (Hosea 6:6 AMP).

God's statement in Hosea 6:6 was mind-blowing to the people of
the day. Their highest expression of religious practice, in that context,
was the sacrificial system of offering bulls, rams, and goats. For God to
say that sacrifice and burnt offerings took a backseat to anything else
was huge. He desired a people who pursued Him and who were deeply
acquainted with Him, not those who simply inserted the religious coin,
turned the dial, and received a vending machine miracle. This attitude
toward God will never sustain a lifestyle of breakthrough. He is interested in people who imitate Him and represent Him.

Sustained breakthrough is not the privilege of those who insert biblical principles just to add to their bottom line in life; rather, sustained
breakthrough is the inheritance of every believer who earnestly desires
to see the character of Jesus Christ accurately represented on the earth.

A FAMINE OF THE KNOWLEDGE OF GOD

Gaining more and more information about God does not develop
breakthrough faith; it is built out of divine encounter with Him. It
is the knowledge of God's character and nature invites us into these
encounters. Sadly, there has been a famine of the knowledge of God in
the contemporary church today. This statement may initially sound odd
due to the amount of Christian content that is circulating on the global
scale. Information about God is not lacking; however, the revelation
that ushers people into encounters with the Person of God is becoming scarce.

Preachers and teachers deliver solid Bible-based principles week after
week in their sermons. After all, they are simply flowing in sync with
what has always been done. But what if God wanted to invite us into a
new wineskin, break the mold of how it's always been done, and bring us

into the place I described in the previous chapter—where deep relationship with Him produces imitation of His character that yields sustained breakthrough in our lives. This is what we are pressing into.

I say "pressing" here because there is resistance as we do this. There is a contrary flow in the body of Christ today. The following passage describes the famine of our day:

> *Hear the word of the Lord, you children of Israel, for the Lord brings a charge against the inhabitants of the land: "There is no truth or mercy or knowledge of God in the land"* (Hosea 4:1).

Gaining more and more information about God does not develop breakthrough faith; it is built out of divine encounter with Him.

There was a lot of knowledge about God in the land during the time of Hosea. People were putting religious principles into practice all of the time. We know this because God consistently reprimands the people for applying principles without pursuing Him. This is key. Our faith is not in a set of principles; it is in a Person.

You may be wondering, "How do I actually receive this knowledge of God?" Scripture gives some powerful direction: *"There is no faithfulness, love, pity and mercy, or knowledge of God [from personal experience with Him] in the land"* (Hosea 4:1 AMP). We know God intimately when we have personal experience with Him. The words in our Bibles were never meant to remain just words and stories. Scripture was never purposed to bloat the brain, filling it up with concepts about God. I pray by the end of this chapter, that all of us would start reading the Bible differently, with a heightened expectation that what is recorded in those pages is available to each one of us today.

Scripture reveals our inheritance of encounter. Every encounter someone enjoyed with God in Scripture is either available to us today or exceedable by us. Old Testament encounters with God's Presence, glory, and power should never be a believer's high watermark for what is available in his or her relationship with God today. Those patriarchs, prophets, kings, and priests enjoyed God under a glorious but nevertheless inferior covenant in the Old Testament (see 2 Cor. 3:7-18). How much more is available to us who have been cleansed by the precious blood of Jesus, adopted into the Father's family, and have the very Spirit of God living within us? We are now partakers of the new and living way (see Heb. 10:20)! These intimate encounters with God reveal who He is in greater measure and bring us into the place of divine friendship that Jesus talked about in John 15.

JESUS GIVES BLANK CHECKS TO HIS FRIENDS

If you abide in Me, and My words abide in you, you will ask what you desire, and it shall be done for you (John 15:7).

When our faith is wrapped up in Jesus being glorified and the Father's nature being revealed, we have a blank check to ask whatever we will in the place of prayer—and expect results! We are licensed not only to ask for whatever we desire, but we can actually expect our requests to be granted when we are asking out of a place of abiding intimacy with Jesus. Immediately, our thoughts run to the appropriate "boundary lines" of this promise. Does this mean we can ask *anything* of God in the place of prayer. Absolutely. It is legal to approach God with requests for the impossible, the outlandish, the extreme. (Again, pending that the requests are in agreement with His Word and His nature.)

Scripture reveals our inheritance of encounter.

Will we always get what we desire or ask for? No. This is where our maturity is tested and revealed. This is where the true friends of God are made known. The true friends of God trust His "no," understanding that His "no" is paving the way for an ultimate and greater "yes." He longs to say "yes" to our prayers, but the key is in saying "yes" to the things that will bring His world to this one and establish His Kingdom here upon the earth.

The wonderful thing about friendship with God is that we start praying like Him. We begin to pray the very things He would pray, and we do this not because He is controlling us like a robot or because He is removing our personal desires. We do this because our desires are actually shaped in God's Presence and reflect the nature of the One we are enjoying closeness with. Bill Johnson makes a fantastic comment about the context of John 15, explaining, "Surrounding their promotion to *friendship*, Jesus gave His disciples this amazing list of promises. Each promise was a blank check they were to live by and use throughout their lives for the expansion of the Kingdom."[22]

The problem is that many who embrace or teach distorted "faith" doctrines have ended up shipwrecked in their own faith. They became extremely disillusioned because they put all of the "faith principles" to work but never saw any results—or at least consistent results. The problem is that faith became me-centric instead of God-centric. Faith was not vitally linked to an intimate friendship with God or a conviction to see the name of Jesus exalted in the earth. Rather, it was a spiritual tool to get one's personal needs met.

God is inviting us into a dimension of faith where we take Jesus' radical words seriously and start filling out these "blank checks" in prayer. However, there is one condition to experiencing this measure of breakthrough faith, where we become eligible to live out this supernatural "blank check" lifestyle. Jesus told the disciples,

> *No longer do I call you servants, for a servant does not know what his master is doing; but I have called you friends, for all things that I heard from My Father I have made known to you* (John 15:15).

The friends of God are able to fill in blank checks with their prayers. Why is friendship with Him so important? Jesus explained it in John 15:15. Friends know what the Master is doing at all times. Friends are close to Jesus and, in turn, close to the Father. Friends see the movement of the Father in the activity and works of the Son. Friends hear the life-giving words of the Father as they spend time listening to what the Son says. When our hearts burn for closeness with God and we start discovering who He is through the model of Jesus Christ, our prayers cannot help but be shaped by these realities. We start praying what we know to be in agreement with who our Father is because we are being shaped by Jesus' character, and nature through our friendship with Him. Imitation is taking place through intimacy.

> **Our desires are actually shaped in God's Presence and reflect the nature of the One we are enjoying closeness with.**

THE POWER OF PURSUIT

When God is our great pursuit and His words are our nourishment, we can then be confident that when we ask for something in the place of prayer, in faith, there is strong likelihood that it will come to pass. We can boldly expect our faith to produce what we are asking and believing for because our faith is in alignment with the desires of the One we live to pursue.

Conversely, if our life pursuit is wrapped up in prideful self-fulfillment, and we place God in the passenger seat, then faith becomes a tool to enhance this self-pursuit. This is simply not faith, and, as a result, has no guarantees attached to it. Faith is not a principle for self-gain; it is a lifestyle that establishes opportunities for our Great Pursuit—God—to receive great glory in the earth.

The breakthroughs and miracles we once pursued as primary are not being cast aside, but instead are becoming the by-products of a lifestyle sold out to the knowledge of God. Prophetic teacher R. Loren Sandford comments, "Signs and wonders are not the goal. They are the result. Well-being is not the focus but rather the outcome. Prosperity is not the pursuit but rather the gift of a loving Father and the fruit of integrity. Glory must not be the longing in our hearts. It is instead God's response to a people who have become intimate with Him at the level of heart and character."[28]

We pursue the knowledge of God and love Him because He first loved us (see 1 John 4:19). We pursue Him because we have long been the object of His pursuit. For the ones love struck by Jesus, the prayers that flow from their hearts and mouths will reflect His nature and carry His creative power. We are not simply praying in agreement with God, but are actually giving voice to His very desires through our voices. You and I have the glorious privilege, through our faith, to give visible expression to the very desires of almighty God in the earth. Intimacy shows us God's heart and faith releases God's will. *very important*

This is the relationship that births true breakthrough faith! Just imagine a church where the people prayed—and they consistently received what they asked for and declared! This is the shift that is currently taking place in the body of Christ today. God is bringing His people out of the up-and-down cycle, where we experience answered prayer one day and defeat the next. He is summoning His people into a lifestyle of consistent breakthrough. The path to this walk of sustained power is pursuing the knowledge of God, and with that knowledge, we build a deep, personal friendship with the Creator of all and Savior of our souls.

**Intimacy shows us God's heart and
faith releases God's will.**

POINT OF BREAKTHROUGH

*God is a Person, not a set of principles. By developing intimate
friendship with Jesus, our prayers are shaped to reflect God's
nature. This authorizes us to ask whatever we want from
God and actually expect that these prayers will be heard and
answered—because they express His character and will.*

~~~

RECOMMENDED READING

Desiring God by John Piper

Knowing God by J.I. Packer

Knowledge of the Holy by A.W. Tozer

7

THE RADICAL QUEST

~~~

*Yet indeed I also count all things loss for the excellence
of the knowledge of Christ Jesus my Lord, for whom I
have suffered the loss of all things, and count them as
rubbish, that I may gain Christ.* —PHILIPPIANS 3:8

The apostle Paul was not just seeking after principles for victory, success, and breakthrough. Paul's great quest and radical pursuit was the very face of God revealed in the Person of Jesus Christ. He was undeniably a man of great faith. In fact, he was such a powerful preacher that he could say with confidence that *"my speech and my preaching were not with persuasive words of human wisdom, but in demonstration of the Spirit and of power, that your faith should not be in the wisdom of men but in the power of God"* (1 Cor. 2:4-5).

He did not merely deliver rhetoric or eloquent words. When Paul preached, his words carried and released pure power. This world changer did not peddle teaching tapes on the Five Steps to a Miracle or Twenty Tips to Get Your Breakthrough. He was not driven by principles, although he obviously lived by them. If anyone had a list of "power principles" to share, it surely would have been Paul. Yet we watch many people today—both church leaders and everyday believers—trying to experience sustained victory by simply using faith formulas or seeking quick-fix solutions. Sadly, they are not enjoying the results they chase after in any kind of consistent manner.

Paul did not live his Christian life to pursue a breakthrough or a blessing; these were not the end goals of faith for him. Jesus was His ultimate pursuit. Beholding the face of God in the Person of Christ was the fuel for Paul's zeal and fire. The very thing that qualified Paul to enjoy a supernatural lifestyle was simple—His radical quest was knowing the very Person of Jesus Christ, not simply enjoying the blessings of Jesus.

> **Paul's great quest and radical pursuit was the very face of God revealed in the Person of Jesus Christ.**

As a result, God used him mightily, releasing signs, wonders, and dynamic miracles through his life and ministry. Acts 19:11 shows us that God was *"performing extraordinary miracles by the hands of Paul* (NASB)." This language baffles me. Extraordinary miracles suggests that there was a level beyond ordinary miracles that Paul somehow stepped into. Bill Johnson describes it this way: "It's amazing that the miracle realm can become so normal that Luke (in Acts 19:11), under the inspiration of the Holy Spirit, had to create a separate category to describe new miracles. They operate at a higher level of mystery, anointing and authority."[24]

Is this idea of "extraordinary miracles" unbiblical, or was Paul experiencing what Jesus prophesied in John 14 concerning greater works? We will cover this in greater depth later on. I propose Paul was no spiritual superhero, but simply a man with a heart that burned for closeness with Christ. The apostle was so gloriously immersed in the Presence of God that the natural outflow of such intimacy was a whole new level of supernatural demonstration in his life.

This is truly a powerful example of sustained supernatural faith! A lifestyle of breakthrough is strongly implied, as there is a noticeable transition from miracles, signs, and wonders to what Luke defines as extraordinary. Remember, attempting to simply use biblical principles without pursuing the Person of Jesus leads to formalism and religion. Paul did not pursue principles apart from a Person.

HOW DOES THIS WORK IN MY EVERYDAY LIFE?

There are three vital relationships that will empower us to enjoy this breakthrough faith lifestyle. Even though this principle of pursuing the knowledge of God can get us spiritually psyched up, sometimes we are not given concrete instructions on where to go next. The problem is that, in some circles, it is preached without any corresponding action plan. As a result of having no follow-through strategy, our spiritual highs deflate quickly. You may be thinking, "How do I actually pursue and experience this 'knowledge of God' you are writing about?" It all begins with understanding how to interact and relate with the Triune God.

In the following three points, we are going to take one of the most mysterious, complex, and historically confounding truths of Scripture—the Trinity—and practically discover how we are called to relate with God by using the Trinity as our model.

Intentionally Develop a Relationship with the Holy Spirit

This is more important than most of us realize. In this hour, God is inviting His people to focus on the Holy Spirit like never before. Most importantly, the Holy Spirit is God on the earth. Remember, the Father and the Son are in Heaven. The Spirit is the One we have been given as our Helper this side of eternity. If this is indeed the case, it should not surprise us that the enemy has attempted to attach so much controversy to the Holy Spirit. If the devil can prevent us from enjoying relationship with the Holy Spirit, he can successfully rob our interaction with God of its intimacy, closeness, and enjoyment.

**Attempting to simply use biblical principles
without pursuing the Person of Jesus
leads to formalism and religion.**

The Holy Spirit is not just a dispenser of miracles or the sovereign giver of spiritual gifts. While such are true realities, they do not define nor encapsulate His fullness. He is a Person who is just as much God as the Father and the Son. Jesus calls Him the "advantage," noting that it was actually to the disciples' benefit that Jesus departed so He could send the Holy Spirit to dwell with them and be in them. He stated, *"Nevertheless I tell you the truth. It is to your advantage that I go away; for if I do not go away, the Helper will not come to you"* (John 16:7).

There are so many incredible books and teachings out there on the Holy Spirit right now,[25] so rather than try to repeat what has already been written, I simply want to encourage you to be intentional about developing a relationship with the Holy Spirit. He is the only way we will ever truly know God. He is the gateway to knowing the Son, and, ultimately, the catalyst to imitating the Father. Paul calls the Holy Spirit the Spirit of Jesus Christ (see Phil. 1:19). When we intentionally pursue relationship with the Holy Spirit, He reveals Jesus to us and, as a result, we get to know God the Father in a greater way.

Behold the Face of Jesus Christ

The "face" of Jesus refers to the example of Jesus. Everything about the Son of God should be regarded as precious to us, from His words to His works to His actions. We are given eyes to truly see who Jesus was and what He was like only through the enabling of the Holy Spirit.

The Holy Spirit makes us aware of our need for Christ to begin with, as such a decision is utterly impossible without His divine intervention. Once we are saved, however, the Holy Spirit has a strategic mission for believers—one that we often neglect. The Holy Spirit's agenda is *not* to keep us focused on the *method* of redemption (the cross) but on the *inheritance* of redemption—the unveiling of the Person, example, and model of Jesus Christ. Jesus said of Him, *"He will glorify Me, for He will take of what is Mine and declare it to you. All things that the Father has are Mine. Therefore I said that He will take of Mine and declare it to you"* (John 16:14-15).

The Holy Spirit opens our eyes to Jesus in a fresh way. By no means am I downgrading the cross or the redemptive work of Christ here. He is forever the worthy Lamb who is eternally deserving of our worship for that significant and utterly spectacular act—Calvary. However, while living on the earth, we must tap into what this act of redemption has provided for us so that we can steward this glorious inheritance. Because we have received the *same* Spirit that was in Christ, we have been invited and empowered to fulfill Jesus' words: *"As the Father has sent Me, I also send you"* (John 20:21). Right after giving the disciples this commission, *"He breathed on them, and said to them, 'Receive the Holy Spirit'"* (John 20:22).

The Holy Spirit gives us revelation of who Jesus is on earth and what He accomplished because of the Spirit's anointing in His life. In return, the same Spirit empowers you and me to model what we see demonstrated in Jesus' example. However, the main emphasis is not just in the demonstration. Many today rightly focus on doing what Jesus did, but we must begin by looking at who Jesus was and who He ultimately revealed. Everything Jesus did was intentional about revealing a Person—Father God. This is the essence of what it means to follow the model of Jesus.

The outcome of us doing His supernatural works and walking in sustained breakthrough is never enhanced comfort. It is not just about needs being met, although He is full of compassion and love. It is not just so we can live healthy and whole. While we celebrate the immediate and direct blessing the supernatural works of Jesus have in our lives and in the lives of others, the main emphasis is always the unveiling of the Father.

> **The Holy Spirit's agenda is *not* to keep us focused on the *method* of redemption (the cross) but on the *inheritance* of redemption—the unveiling of the Person, example, and model of Jesus Christ.**

Encounter the Father

This brings us to the Father. It is amazing how, apart from the Holy Spirit, we really cannot see or know the Father. The Holy Spirit is the great revealer of Jesus Christ, and it is the face, words, works, and model of Jesus that all usher us into an encounter with the Father.

Even though Philip was staring at the very answer to his question, he still asked for Jesus to show him the Father. Jesus responded by saying,

> *Do you not believe that I am in the Father, and the Father in Me? The words that I speak to you I do not speak on My own authority; but the Father who dwells in Me does the works. Believe Me that I am in the Father and the Father in Me, or else believe Me for the sake of the works themselves* (John 14:10-11).

These are some of the most loaded words in all of Scripture. How do we respond to them? Bill Johnson often comments that any revelation of God the Father that contradicts what Jesus revealed about Him should be called into question. The words and works of Jesus are, scripturally speaking, the most accurate representation and unveiling of the Father's likeness, character, and nature available to mankind.

> *Christ is the exact likeness of the unseen God* (Colossians 1:15 TLB).

> *The Son radiates God's own glory and expresses the very character of God* (Hebrews 1:3 NLT).

If we want to make the pursuit of the knowledge of God practical, this is how I would sum it up: first, we intentionally cultivate and develop a relationship with Holy Spirit. He is God on earth and the chief revealer of Jesus Christ. Second, as the Holy Spirit reveals Jesus to us, those questions about who God is and what His will is are constantly answered. Jesus is not only our redeemer, but He is also the revealer. He shows us the Father. In fact, He is the exclusive representative of the Father, as He makes it crystal clear that *"no one comes to the Father except through Me"* (John 14:6). This statement is both redemptive and revelatory in nature. No one can get to the Father except through Jesus, the Messianic bridge-builder; and no one can understand, encounter, and intimately know what the Father is like except through the revelation and model of Jesus.

That Scripture does not lose its relevance once we enter the Kingdom. If anything, the treasure trove of the knowledge of God truly opens up once we cross Calvary's bridge into the Kingdom and begin the eternal journey of knowing this glorious God. Jesus follows up by saying, *"If you really knew Me, you would know My Father as well. From now on, you do know Him. You've even seen Him!"* (John 14:7 MSG). When we see the Father and know Him *as He is*, we become ready to imitate Him. This is what positioned the apostle Paul to walk in the supernatural dimension of breakthrough that we read about in the New Testament.

> **The words and works of Jesus are, scripturally speaking, the most accurate representation and unveiling of the Father's likeness, character, and nature available to mankind.**

INTIMACY, IMITATION, AND BREAKTHROUGH FAITH

This chapter has been a radical call to pursue the foundation of breakthrough faith—the knowledge of God. Jesus' blood removed every single barrier, obstacle, and hindrance to us knowing the Father. It's only when we know God that we are able to know how to demonstrate our faith because we become positioned to imitate the One we are intimate with. When we imitate God, speaking how He speaks and releasing His solutions over the obstacles in our lives, we start walking out a supernatural lifestyle of breakthrough faith. Again, it all begins with knowing Him and this is where we have missed it.

The devil has done everything he possibly can to prevent the body of Christ from pursuing the knowledge of God. He is well aware that when our eyes lock with the Lover of Our Souls, our hearts will burn and our taste for anything less than God Himself will be utterly ruined.

We cannot misunderstand the purpose of salvation. If we miss the goal of the Christian experience, we will consistently fall short of enjoying a lifestyle of sustained victory through exercising faith. Salvation is not simply about going to Heaven some day. Salvation is not *just* having a relationship with Jesus. I know this may sound shocking, but hear me out for a moment—these are all blessings and by-products of salvation. They are the wonderful benefits of salvation. Salvation and eternal life begin with this fundamental cornerstone, as defined by Jesus Himself: *"And this is eternal life, that they may know You, the only true God, and Jesus Christ whom You have sent"* (John 17:3).

To know God is to relate to Him and relate with Him—accurately. When we assume salvation is about relationship first, then there is a strong likelihood that we will attempt to relate with a God we do not know, do not really desire to know, or know inaccurately. The knowledge of God actually fuels our relationship with Him. To relate with God and enjoy deep communion with Him is to be transformed into His likeness. To be transformed into His likeness is to imitate Him, and to imitate God is to walk in breakthrough faith.

Breakthrough faith is about knowing God and behaving like Him through imitation. The Lord is summoning us to participate in a great quest that rivals any adventure our minds could possibly conceive. Remember, the deeper the intimacy with God, the more accurate the imitation. This is the starting place of breakthrough faith—a people who deeply know, accurately imitate, and powerfully represent King Jesus in the earth.

> **When our eyes lock with the Lover of Our Souls, our hearts will burn and our taste for anything less than God Himself will be utterly ruined.**

In the next section we will continue to build on this pillar of the knowledge of God. God's acts reveal His character and, in turn, demonstrate His ability. We celebrate that God is able; but to walk in breakthrough faith, we must combine two vital revelations: God is able and God is willing!

POINT OF BREAKTHROUGH

The most radical quest of our lives is pursuing the knowledge of God through intimacy and friendship with Him. This is what made the apostle Paul a dynamic ambassador of the Kingdom. More than pursuing miracles or breakthrough, his single radical pursuit was the very face of God as revealed in the Person of Jesus Christ. To know God is to desire deep friendship with Him. Such intimacy produces imitation, and by imitating God, we walk in a sustained lifestyle of breakthrough faith.

~~

RECOMMENDED READING

After God's Own Heart by Mike Bickle

Drawing Near by John Bevere

Face to Face With God by Bill Johnson

ABLE AND WILLING

~~~

Appropriating faith is not believing that God can, but that God will. —F.F. Bosworth[26]

The generation that marries both the truths of God's ability *and* His willingness will walk in supernatural breakthrough as their norm, not as the exception. The expression of "normal Christianity" will once again be followed by signs, wonders, miracles, and radical supernatural demonstrations of the Kingdom of God because a people decided to believe that the God who is able is *also willing*. The following section is intentionally divided up to cover first the ability of God and then conclude by exploring His willingness. One revelation without the other will not suffice, and, unfortunately, will lead us into short-circuited faith.

There are entire "faith" groups out there who present a God whose willingness is unlimited. He is willing to do everything from heal your body to giving you a shiny new Bentley, to providing you with a wardrobe of Armani suits. Nice things are not the issue here; the problem is when stuff becomes the focus of our faith and God's willingness is preached *without* boundaries.

This is why I am first presenting the section on the ability of God. God's ability, as revealed throughout Scripture, provides boundaries for what we are licensed to believe Him for. Boundaries in God's Kingdom are not restrictive; rather, they are protective. God is not out to limit us in how we exercise our faith. If anything, God wants to upgrade our understanding of what He is able to do, and believe Him for the "greater works" that Jesus spoke of in John 14:12. The key is found in believing for the things that lie within Heaven's specified perimeters.

> **The generation that marries both the truths of God's ability *and* His willingness will walk in supernatural breakthrough as their norm, not as the exception.**

When we believe that the God who is able to speak galaxies into existence is the *same* God who is also willing to perform the impossible on our behalf, this faith produces limitless results. So here is my question: Are you ready to experience an upgraded Christian life? If your answer is yes, then let's dive in and explore God's ability, God's willingness, and the incredible power that is released when we put these two revelations together.

8

THE ABILITY OF GOD

~~

Behold, I am the Lord, the God of all flesh. Is there
anything too hard for Me? —JEREMIAH 32:27

God is able. In this section we are going to discover how placing our faith in God's unlimited ability is so much more than merely believing He can or might do something. To walk in breakthrough faith, we need to believe that the able God is also *willing*. This section is designed to whet your spiritual appetite. By exploring what is revealed in Scripture, my desire is that your paradigm of what God is able to do will dramatically and supernaturally shift. Remember, before we set out to explore God's willingness, we need to have a clear picture of what He is *able* to do.

Sadly, the statement "God is able" has become a cheesy, weightless Christian platitude that is often said at the wrong time and delivered without any follow-through.

Going through a difficult time? No worries. *God is able.*

Face to face with a terminal disease? Hang in there. *God is able.*

Is your family falling apart? Keep pressing through. *God is able.*

Have you fallen prey to layoffs, plunging stocks, depleting retirement funds, and a shifting economy? Keep your head up. *God is able.*

This is not meant to be insensitive toward those who are going through struggles; we just need to start getting real with God and with each other. The belief that God is able is absolutely foundational and fundamental to cultivating breakthrough faith. The problem is not so much in the statement of fact, but rather in the definition we have come to assign this phrase. Basically, we are saying that He *can* do something—however, whether or not He *will* is a whole other story.

> ## To walk in breakthrough faith, we need to believe that the able God is also *willing*.

The problem is that we level God's ability by bringing it down to earth. We bring Him down to mortal terms, and the "miracles" we assign to His supernatural ability are, oftentimes, a joke. They are subpar exploits compared to what the almighty, omnipotent God is truly capable of accomplishing in our lives and throughout the earth. Where is the generation who will dare to gaze upon His glorious face and behold the One who is truly able *"to accomplish infinitely more than we might ask or think"* (Eph. 3:20 NLT)?

In twenty-first-century Christianity, it seems like God is basically able to do whatever we can do. He is able to pay off loans for our church buildings. He is able to grow the youth group. He is able to give us jobs. He is able to pay our bills. He is able to get us out of debt. He is able to modify our behavior—but only to a degree. When we experience one of these victories, we celebrate and call it God. There is nothing wrong with extending credit to Him, as apart from Him we can truly do nothing (see John 15:5). But I do take issue with us labeling everything as a miracle, for by doing so we begin to reduce miracles to what can be accomplished by a combination of wisdom, the fruit of the Spirit, and divine strategy.

The fact that we are able to take our next breath is, in part, a miracle. However, we need to realign our concept of the miraculous with what we read about in the accounts of Scripture. When it comes to what almighty God is able to do, all of us are due for a *belief upgrade*. It is not about acquiring more and more faith; it is about having a greater vision for what the faith God has *already* given us is able to produce. This takes place when our source manual for what God is able to do becomes His Word alone.

I don't care how old the testimonies contained in Scripture are; and I don't care how outlandish some of them sound to our rational, contemporary minds. I don't care about the alleged infrequency of "those kinds of miracles" happening in our country or world today. Such facts are quite irrelevant to me. Indeed, these facts are the very stumbling blocks that thwart us from pressing in to receive, experience, and release the supernatural realities that Scripture entitles us to. The Bible is a wonderful book of testimony. It reveals what God has done, and if God has done it, then He can surely do it again. No wonder the psalmist wrote, *"My soul keeps Your testimonies, and I love them exceedingly"* (Ps. 119:167).

The Bible alone must become our benchmark for what we can legally believe God for. Not a doctrine. Not a church or denomination. Not a spiritual leader. Not a friend or family member. Not a Christian book or a passionately delivered sermon. Scripture is *the* foundation when it comes to providing a sure list of what we are licensed to believe God for. We believe based on *His* ability as revealed through the pages of *His* Word.

UPGRADING OUR PARADIGM OF GOD'S ABILITY

God is raising up a generation of men and women who are deeply intimate with God like Paul was, and who, in turn, become conduits for *unusual* and *extraordinary* miracles. If Paul performed such miraculous exploits, you and I are able to do likewise. It does not require some faith upgrade; if anything, we need to enlarge our concept of what faith is able to do!

However, we will never walk in the greater works of John 14:12 or experience the unusual or extraordinary miracles described in Acts 19:11-12 if we continue to believe that God's miraculous ability simply covers building programs, attendance growth, financial problems, and integrating discipline into our lives.

> ## The Bible alone must become our benchmark
> ## for what we can legally believe God for.

The problem is that many of us have lived disconnected from the fullness of God's ability because, for some reason, we have relegated His more supernatural activities and works to the realm of "Bible times." The same God who moved miraculously back in "Bible times" is still moving today. He never changed! The writer of Hebrews says, *"For whoever would come near to God must [necessarily] believe that God exists..."* (Heb. 11:6 AMP). If you are reading this book, then you surely have some concept or belief that God does indeed exist. That He is real. I want you to take it a step further now. Not only do you need to believe that there is a real Person called God *out there somewhere*, but you need to believe that He exists *as...*

What do I mean by saying that He *exists as...*? God's works reveal God's ability. He heals and thus reveals His identity *as* healer. He delivers, thereby confirming that He is the deliverer. He saves and is thus the Savior. He exists, absolutely, but He also exists *as* healer, deliverer, Savior, restorer, fortress, strong tower, friend, Lover of Our Souls, and the list endlessly goes on and on.

It is now time to start upgrading our belief system. When we get honest with the Bible, the Holy Spirit wonderfully rocks our paradigm of God's limitless ability. Take this opportunity to review some of the unusual miracles and works that God performed throughout Scripture. This is only a small sampling, but I intentionally selected some of the more radical ones for the very purpose of unboxing God's ability in your life:

- God is able to create everything from nothing (see Gen. 1:1-2).

- God is able to create worlds using words (see Gen. 1:3; Heb. 1:3).

- God is able to part oceans, redeem entire nations, and drown the armies of His enemies (see Exod. 14).

- God is able to bring fortified walls crumbling to the ground through the power of a shout (see Josh. 6:16-17).

- God is able to make the sun stand still (see Josh. 10:1-15).

The same God who moved miraculously back in "Bible times" is still moving today.

- God is able to give offspring to the barren, aged, and, on one occasion, the virgin (see the example of Sarah in Hebrews 11:11, Rebekah in Genesis 25:21, Hannah in 1 Samuel 1:2, 19-20, Elizabeth in Luke 1:7, 57-58, and Mary in Luke 1:26-38).

- God is able to restore everything the devil has stolen or destroyed…and pay it back with interest (see Job 42:12-17).

- God is able to release resurrection power through a dead man's bones (see 2 Kings 13:21).

- God is able to save and transform an entire city (see Jon. 3:5-10).

- God is able to shut down our programs and release His Presence in such a weighty, powerful measure that everyone falls to the ground (see 2 Chron. 5:13-14).

- God is able to raise the dead…even after being four days in the grave (see John 11:17-44).

- God is able to supernaturally reattach severed limbs (see Luke 22:51).

- God is able to send a detachment of soldiers to the ground simply by announcing His identity (see John 18:6).

- God is able to birth a movement that would transform and shape history by using strange babblings, a sound from Heaven, a rushing wind, fire, and a group of men acting like they were drunk (see Acts 2:1-13).

- God is able to shake buildings through unified prayer (see Acts 4:31).

- God is able to supernaturally teleport someone from one geographical region to another (see Acts 8:39-40).

- God is able to destroy the power of death...by dying on the cross (see Heb. 2:14).

This list could continue on for an entire book. In fact, John concludes his Gospel account by writing, *"And there are also many other things that Jesus did, which if they were written one by one, I suppose that even the world itself could not contain the books that would be written"* (John 21:25).

So what does this list of miracles mean for you and me today? Let me follow it up with an example from the New Testament. In Acts 14:8-10 Paul releases supernatural healing to a crippled man. The people are so astounded by this act that they begin to herald him as some type of god. Paul's response in verse 15 reminds us that as carriers of God's Presence and power, we are able to perform the same miraculous works. He says, *"Men, why are you doing these things? We also are men with the same nature as you."* Paul was clearly affirming his humanity and normalcy. Paul was a man—who was anointed. Elijah was a man—who just happened to be anointed. Peter was a man—who also was anointed. And we today are men and women of God—whom God empowers in the same way that He anointed men and women of long ago, carrying the same Presence and power. Anointed to do *what*? Represent God by showing the world what He is able to do.

POINT OF BREAKTHROUGH

One of the first steps to walking out a lifestyle of breakthrough faith is believing that God is able—and specifically identifying what Scripture says He is able to do. These are the works we are anointed to perform as His ambassadors and representatives.

~~

RECOMMENDED READING

Christ the Healer by F.F. Bosworth

Ever Increasing Faith by Smith Wigglesworth

John G. Lake: Complete Collection of His Teaching compiled by Roberts Liardon

9

OVERCOMING THE BARRIERS
TO BELIEVING

~~

Jesus Christ is the same yesterday, today, and forever. Do not be carried about with various and strange doctrines. —HEBREWS 13:8-9

Before we discuss God's willingness, it is necessary to confront two major barriers to believing that He is both able and willing to do what He promised. The author of Hebrews is quick to remind us that there are "various and strange" doctrines that try to assault the truth that Jesus Christ is the same yesterday, today, and forever.

It is vital that we read Scripture through an "available now" lens. Otherwise, the biblical accounts merely remain good stories rather than serve as invitations for us to stare down the impossible with confidence—just like the great men and women of old did. God has not changed since Genesis 1:1. Instead, somewhere along the line, our idea of what God was able to do shifted.

We have limited His ability by embracing two barriers: legalism and cessationism. These concepts must be practically acknowledged and dealt with if we are going to believe that God is actually able to perform the extraordinary and supernatural...today.

It is vital that we read Scripture through an "available now" lens.

BARRIER #1: LEGALISM

Christianity without demonstration is useless. Revivalist Leonard Ravenhill put it best by suggesting that the world outside is not waiting for a new definition of Christianity, it's waiting for a new demonstration of Christianity.[27] Legalism forbids a believer from venturing beyond the known and exploring other possibilities for fear of going "off the deep end" into false doctrine, sin, or perhaps even worse. Legalism is not concerned about being honest with Scripture; it is concerned with upholding a particular interpretation of Scripture. And if we steer away from this one certain interpretation of Scripture, perhaps gleaned from a denomination or pastor or background, we are drifting into heresy. We need to confront and break this lie, head on.

This is not a call to question orthodox theological doctrine: the virgin birth, the deity of Christ, the atonement, the black and whites of what defines sin, the infallibility and inerrancy of Scripture, etc. I am addressing legalism in a very specific context here—legalism that prevents us from pressing in for the impossible by upholding an image of a God who moved back then but does not move in power today.

The religious disease of legalism manifests in many different ways. The legalistic spirit responsible for "encouraging" people to "clean up their act" before God fully accepts them is the same motivating spirit that fuels cessationism (we will explore this in just a minute). In fact, legalism and cessationism work in tandem. The devil uses legalism as a vehicle for bondage. It keeps us trapped in an incorrect way of thinking, preventing us from exploring other options concerning God's supernatural ability. Legalism says, "You can't do this" or "You can only do that." When applied to God, it maintains that God can do this or that, and yes, it audaciously states that God can't do anything supernatural any longer. It truly is a diabolical system of restraint.

When it comes to exercising our faith, we had better believe that the enemy is seeking to restrain the body of Christ from believing that the great God who worked wonders back in Bible times still works wonders today. His objective is to keep us trapped in the snare of cessationism. Legalism represents the bars that keep us in the prison of this false belief concerning God's ability.

BARRIER #2: CESSATIONISM

Cessationism is a religiously packaged deception that is robbing so many believers of walking in sustained breakthrough, victory, and supernatural power. This theological sounding word describes a belief system that rejects a modern, normative supernatural experience for the average believer. One official definition of cessationism is that "the Charismatic gifts were intended to cease after the New Testament."[28]

A cessationist perspective believes that select spiritual gifts are no longer in operation (tongues, miracles, and prophecy), signs and wonders were exclusive to the apostles' time and ceased when the Bible was compiled and canonized, and that the twenty-first-century church should live beneath the supernatural experience exemplified by both Jesus Christ and the disciples in the first-century church. In short, cessationism in its purest form believes that God does not normally perform the miraculous today except, occasionally, by divine providence.

There are some dear brothers and sisters in the body of Christ—many of whom are leaders—who embrace this perspective. I honor them. I have gleaned a great deal of revelation from their ministries and believe they have much to sow into an often-imbalanced Spirit-filled community. I am not pointing condemning fingers at those who adopt a cessationist perspective, branding them as "less-than Christians." This is not a matter of spiritual elitism. Nor is it, "If you practice this gift of the Holy Spirit" you are more spiritually mature, a better Christian, etc. This is not about being better or more mature than the next believer; it's about achieving maximum Kingdom effectiveness in the strategic moment we have been given in history.

THE ENEMY'S WAR ON A BELIEVING CHURCH

Cessationism wars against the fundamental purpose of the church, which is to enforce the divine power and Kingdom authority of Jesus Christ in the earth, *"to the intent that now the manifold wisdom of God might be made known by the church to the principalities and powers in the heavenly places"* (Eph. 3:10). The church is God's vehicle for dispelling darkness, demolishing demonic strongholds, and extinguishing every scheme of satan that presently tarnishes this planet.

The devil has made cessationism an issue because He recognizes the threat that a faith-filled church poses to his domain of darkness. Remember, Jesus added no caveats or expiration dates to his original Kingdom mandate for the church in Matthew 16:18-19:

> *On this rock I will build My church, and the gates of Hades shall not prevail against it. And I will give you the keys of the kingdom of heaven, and whatever you bind on earth will be bound in heaven, and whatever you loose on earth will be loosed in heaven.*

To believe that God no longer supplies miracles as normative is to call Jesus' very definition of the church into question, as He describes a church that is armed with divine vision and supernatural keys of authority. Divine vision sees into the world of Heaven through Scripture—what's present and what's absent. Sickness is absent. Demonic influences are absent. Torment is absent. If such are absent in Heaven, they must be rendered absent on earth. The church is God's enforcement vehicle, anointed to bind or forbid on earth what is already bound and forbidden in Heaven.

Likewise, we are empowered to loose or release on earth that which is already normative in Heaven. Wholeness. Fullness of joy. Peace. Freedom. Health. Liberty. The list is endless and is revealed throughout Scripture. Jesus was not just spouting out arbitrary words in the Lord's Prayer when He gave us the vision of "on earth as it is in Heaven" (see Matt. 6:10). Really, the Lord's Prayer was the vision and Matthew 16 was the commission. The Great Commission reveals how Jesus intended to bring the vision of "on earth as it is in Heaven" to pass through you and me, His body in the earth!

Cessationism deprives believers of fulfilling their destinies as vital members in an advancing, conquering, darkness-defeating church. What blinds us to the deception of cessationism? That tricky old scoundrel called legalism.

> **The church is God's vehicle for dispelling darkness, demolishing demonic strongholds, and extinguishing every scheme of satan that presently tarnishes this planet.**

WHERE CESSATIONISM AND LEGALISM MEET

Many adhere to cessationism not because of a genuine, deep desire to defend and propagate the theory (it is ultimately a theory, not an established doctrine). Instead, they often remain stuck in this system of belief because of the legalistic spirit. Legalism says, "This is how it's always been—if anything challenges what has been done, taught, or preached, reject it as demonic." It is a legalistic paradigm that keeps people believing in cessationism, and not actually exploring what Scripture has to say about a contemporary demonstration of God's supernatural power. As long as the enemy can keep us from pressing into certain biblical truths and contending for them to be released through our lives, he has us right where he wants us: restrained. The devil has no problem with a church of power that does not know it is powerful.

Legalism has no problem with the reality that God is able. This basically believes in God, and we know Scripture says that even the demons believe this reality and tremble (see James 2:19-20). We must begin with a foundation of who God is and what He is able to do. However, such is not the end in and of itself. The truth of God's ability must be married to the compassionate revelation of God's heart of willingness. In other words, God almighty desires to set us up with a divine collision of both

His ability and His willingness. This is what produces the miraculous in us and through us.

Miracles, signs, and wonders were not exclusive to people in Bible times. They were not reserved for the Old Testament patriarchs who lived under the Old Covenant, nor were they limited to the first-century church. The God who was willing to move then is still willing to move today. When we believe that the same God who is able is also willing, we are well on our way to experiencing a lifestyle of breakthrough faith. Let's get ready to finish up this section by putting both of these realities together.

POINT OF BREAKTHROUGH

Two major barriers to believing God are legalism and cessationism; both schools of thought work together. Cessationism believes that the age of God's supernatural power has ended, while legalism keeps people believing theories (such as cessationism) because that is the way it is has always been. The result is a powerless people, not because they are without power, but because they believe power is not available and accessible to them.

~~~

RECOMMENDED READING

The following titles are two user-friendly books on the topics we covered in this chapter, namely the destructive theory of cessationism:

Holy Fire by R.T. Kendall

Authentic Fire by Dr. Michael Brown

10

GOD IS WILLING

~

Then Jesus, moved with compassion, stretched
out His hand and touched him, and said to him,
*"I am willing; be cleansed." —*MARK 1:41

"God is *willing*." This is the revelation that will position us to walk in sustained supernatural power and activate the breakthrough faith God has deposited within us. I pray that your faith has been stirred afresh in God's ability, not simply to build a building, pay off a youth center, or give you a new job. As great as these things are, my heart burns to see believers experience an upgrade in what they believe God is able *and* willing to do.

You know those crazy, wild, amazing things that God did back in the Bible times? I invite you to get a clear picture and visualization of those miracles—to the best of your ability—those extraordinary, supernatural demonstrations of God's glorious power over sickness, demons, death, nature, enemy armies, etc. The God who was able *then* is also able *now*. Not only is He able to do these things in the church and world today, but He is also able to do them in and through you. Not only is He just able to do them, but *He is also willing. The able God is also willing!*

One scriptural foundation that we keep returning to is the truth that Jesus revealed the perfect nature and will of Father God through His time upon the earth. He is both redeemer and revealer. If this is indeed so, consider the following passage and ask yourself the question, "Is Jesus willing?"

> *Now a leper came to Him, imploring Him, kneeling down to Him and saying to Him, "If You are willing, You can make me clean." Then Jesus, moved with compassion, stretched out His hand and touched him, and said to him, "I am willing; be cleansed"* (Mark 1:40-41).

Two things immediately stand out about this account. The first is that the leper obviously recognized Jesus' ability to do the miraculous, otherwise he would not have approached Jesus or made the request for possible healing. There was the acknowledgement of Jesus' ability, which is foundational any time we are longing for Him to show up in our situations. If the leper did not believe that Jesus was able to heal him, he would not have approached Him. It is as simple as that. Belief in Jesus' ability brought the leper to the Miracle Maker.

The able God is also willing!

The second thing that stands out and is worth noting is that the man was not dealing with a bunch of theological ideas or legalistic paradigms. He was not questioning whether or not God still healed and moved today. He was not wrestling over the theological implications of cessationism. The leper was confident in Jesus' ability to heal. However, there was one other step that needed to be resolved for this man, and this is the very issue that many of us confront in the church today: God's willingness.

So here we go. Here are two essential keys to activating our faith through believing that God is willing.

KEY #1: SILENCE THE "UNWORTHINESS" DECEPTION

Our enemy, the devil, will try to convince us that the reason we are dealing with a struggle, trial, or issue is because of our sin. He wants to convince us that we are unworthy to receive breakthrough from God's hand, let alone walk in a lifestyle of sustained victory. "God is angry at you and is teaching you a lesson through your circumstances," he'll suggest. This is a lie. While there are undeniably natural consequences to the bad choices we make, God is not up in Heaven scheming to afflict us with judgment or wrath.

Surely thoughts like this came into the leper's mind as he approached Jesus. After all, the condition of leprosy in Bible times was far more serious than just a mere sickness or infirmity. This man was considered unclean. His ailment identified him and made him an outcast in society. If anyone should have had "worthiness" issues, it would be this leper.

We must model the leper's approach to Jesus: *"Now a leper came to Him"* (Mark 1:40). This is the first step toward breakthrough—we have to come to Jesus, unafraid and unashamed. If we believe that God is actually against us and that Jesus is afflicting us, we will not come to God boldly, as Hebrews 4:16 encourages us to do. The deception of unworthiness has robbed countless lives of not only receiving breakthrough, but of being used to administer breakthrough to others. We will never stand confident that God is willing to do anything for us if we believe that we are unworthy to receive from Him.

We silence the enemy by reminding him of this reality: God's wrath toward sin was satisfied completely at the cross. The key is simply believing it and receiving it by faith. We must believe that He is not angry at us and executing some type of divine retribution upon us. James reminds us that *"every good gift and every perfect gift is from above, and cometh down from the Father of lights, with whom is no variableness, neither shadow of turning"* (James 1:17 KJV). If we have received Christ as Lord and Savior, every ounce of wrath that God had toward sin (never toward us, but always toward sin) was carried and absorbed by Jesus Christ on the cross. Jesus received the brunt of God's wrath so we would never have to.

The apostle Paul knew something about the wrath of God. I am sure the devil tried to condemn him, using his past and history of persecuting the church, bringing it up again and again in order to make him feel worthless. Nevertheless, Paul writes with confidence, *"For our sake He made Christ [virtually] to be sin Who knew no sin, so that in and through Him we might become [endued with, viewed as being in, and examples of] the righteousness of God [what we ought to be, approved and acceptable and in right relationship with Him, by His goodness]"* (2 Cor. 5:21 AMP).

The Living Bible phrases the verse this way: *"For God took the sinless Christ and poured into Him our sins."* It makes sense why there is controversy surrounding the lyrics in Keith Getty and Stuart Townend's modern hymn, "In Christ Alone." There is a line that declares, "On that cross, as Jesus died/The wrath of God was satisfied." A certain denominational group wanted to adjust the lyrics, removing the whole "wrath" bit.[29] The very truth that is under attack in this hymn—the revelation of penal substitutionary atonement—is one of the most liberating truths we could ever wrap our hearts around. In short, God is not mad at any of us.

> **We silence the enemy by reminding him of this reality: God's wrath toward sin was satisfied *completely* at the cross.**

The next time the devil tries to get us to believe, "I'm so sinful. I've messed up so much in my life. I screwed up even today—no wonder this is happening to me. God is repaying me for my sins," I would encourage everyone of us to take an instant trip back to the cross of Calvary— because that is where all of our sin was permanently dealt with. Yes, we admit our sin before the Lord and receive His forgiveness. We repent. We admit wrongdoing. After all, we do this when we make mistakes in relationships with family, friends, and with our spouse.

So when the enemy tries to heap condemnation upon us, trying to convince us of unworthiness, we go back to the cross. We take a trip back to Isaiah 53 and look at the wounded One, for it was upon Him that every iniquity (see Isa. 53:5b), every transgression (see Isa. 53:5a), every sin (see Isa. 53:12), every disease and sickness (see Isa. 53:5d), all torment (see Isa. 53:5c), all judgment, and yes, all the fullness of God's wrath was poured out, as Jesus was in fact smitten by God (see Isa. 53:4)!

The other side of this reality is that while God has no judgment towards those who have been genuinely redeemed by the blood of Jesus, there is still judgment towards sin. This is why it is so important for us to come before the Lord and repent of our sins. We don't do this out of religious obligation or ritual. We genuinely long for a static free intimacy with the Lord. We observe sin as detestable in our lives because it distracts our focus from true beauty, perfect and glory—the face of the Father.

Bill Johnson calls a lifestyle of repentance living "face to face with God." Since repentance is an "about-face," where we turn away from sin and towards God, a lifestyle of repentance is a constant, intentional pursuit of God, while willfully rejecting sin.

Sin is a snare for the believer. This is how the devil gets us to quickly believe the unworthiness deception. When we are living in sin, we are living out of agreement with our new creation identity in Christ. We are called a holy, chosen people. We are set apart. We are filled with the *Holy* Spirit. We are temples of the Living God on Earth. This is our identity. To live in sin is to live beneath this calling. Sin does not change our identity; sadly, it causes us to live out of alignment with it and thus, distanced from our royal privileges and benefits.

God's love towards you is unconditional and eternal. It endures forever. However, sin positions you in a place where the voice of God becomes muffled. It is much easier to believe the enemy's lies if you are willfully pursuing sin, neglecting the Spirit's summons to repent and turn. God longs for you to live face to face with Him. He's not a cruel taskmaster, wanting to impose legalistic restrictions upon you. Every commandment of God is life-giving and life-enhancing.

As you read this, maybe you feel like you have run a million miles away from God. The good news is that, even though you cannot do anything in your own ability to run those million miles back to the Lord, He has already made the first steps towards you. The million-step journey is easy for Him. In fact, He is right there, waiting. Not for your million steps. Not for penance. Not for you to feel condemned for a prolonged period of time before you feel acceptable again. He is simply waiting for repentance. He is looking for eyes that turn away from the vileness of sin and look once again upon the beauty of His countenance.

One of the reasons this unworthiness deception works so well on Christians is because they are living beneath their royal identity in Jesus. Sin does not cancel out this identity; it distracts us from its glorious implications for our lives. For the follower of Jesus to live in sin is to live in a perpetual identity crisis. The redemptive work of the cross declares that you are free from the bondage of sin, delivered from death and translated into a Kingdom of life and resurrection power. To have received this identity, and yet, still pursue sin and the "dead things" of our old lives is to set ourselves up for relentless demonic assault. When we live in sin, we give something for the devil to work with. We not only grant him an in-roads to develop footholds and strongholds in our lives; we also give him endless material to torment us with through his ever loudening voice of condemnation. He uses every sin against us, trying to remind us of our unworthiness before the Lord. How do you defeat him and silence his voice? It's as simple as repenting of your sin, returning to the cross, and reminding yourself: 1) you are officially dead to sin—sin should no longer define your life and identity, and 2) you are alive in Jesus Christ—your sin was actually exchanged for the supernatural, resurrection life and power of Jesus.

Sin should be a foreign land to every disciple of Jesus. It cannot satisfy. Sin is nothing but death. This is why it should feel so alien to us. Will we make mistakes? Yes. Will we become perfect in this lifetime? No. The key is identifying with our status as *in Christ* and dead to sin more than our old life.

Before we became Christians, death, sin, selfishness and lust defined our lives. We were enslaved to these things and didn't even know it. Jesus brought you out of sin and death. In fact, the Bible says He made you a new creation (see 2 Cor. 5:7). Your old life was crucified with Christ. If this is really true, what appeal should a dead life have to those who have been born again and transformed into new creations?

KEY #2: SETTLE THE "IF IT BE THY WILL" QUESTION

Jesus settled what God's will was in a single phrase that He spoke to the leper. The leper, though confident in Jesus' ability, questioned His willingness. Minister and author F.F. Bosworth notes that Jesus corrected this leper's theology.[30] Though he knew that Jesus could make him clean, he was unsure if Jesus was willing to make him clean. Right there, Jesus gave him and us a powerful answer revealing God's will toward sickness, disease, uncleanness, and torment: *"Then Jesus, moved with compassion, stretched out His hand and touched him, and said to him, 'I am willing; be cleansed'"* (Mark 1:41).

There are two extremely clear scriptural blueprints of God's will: Jesus' model and Heaven's culture. First, we have Jesus as the revealer of the Father. Jesus showcased the nature and character of Father God before humanity. If Jesus performed the will of the Father, I propose that the very will of God concerning many different situations and circumstances has been made abundantly clear through Jesus' actions. There is still mystery attached to the sovereign God—lots of it, in fact. But at the same time, Jesus gives us license to believe for many different things with complete confidence and supernatural boldness. Why? Because He did them, which means the Father must will them to be done. He healed. He delivered people from torment, bondage, and oppression. He raised the dead. All of this was part of the Father's will.

The second blueprint for God's will is the culture of Heaven. Returning briefly to Matthew 16:18-19, Jesus made this powerful announcement concerning the purpose and mission of His church—to enforce Heaven's culture in the earth. He stated, *"I will give you the keys of the kingdom of heaven; and whatever you bind on earth shall have been bound in heaven, and whatever you loose on earth shall have been loosed in heaven"* (Matt. 16:19 NASB). Other translations can lead us into confusion, as they almost make it sound like people have some type of commanding power with God.

In other words, if we bind something on earth, our choice directs what Heaven releases, kind of like we are ordering God around. This is a distortion. Heaven models and shapes *our* choices, not the other way around. We bind on earth what has already been bound in Heaven; we are simply being obedient to the blueprint of Heaven. Likewise, we loose or release that which is already loosed in Heaven. We are not imposing our will on God's, but rather taking our place as the enforcers of His will in this world over our circumstances.

There are two extremely clear scriptural blueprints for God's will: Jesus' model and Heaven's culture.

So this begs the question, What is loosed in Heaven? What does the culture look like in God's world? We catch a powerful glimpse in Revelation 21:3-4:

> *And I heard a loud voice from heaven saying, "Behold, the tabernacle of God is with men, and He will dwell with them, and they shall be His people. God Himself will be with them and be their God. And God will wipe away every tear from their eyes; there shall be no more death, nor sorrow, nor crying. There shall be no more pain, for the former things have passed away."*

Immediately, the reaction is, "Yeah, but that's Heaven!" Our theology has been shaped by a futuristic perspective that disregards the present relevance of the Lord's Prayer—"on earth as it is in Heaven." The blessings and rewards and atmosphere of God's world were never meant to simply be cherished in the afterlife alone. Heaven is our destination; but this moment, this hour, and this planet are our assignments. Jesus gave us some pretty specific instructions on how to complete this assignment, revealing God's will for your life and mine. He taught us to pray, *"Your kingdom come. Your will be done on earth as it is in heaven"* (Matt. 6:10).

Why are we not seeing more of Heaven on earth then? It has nothing to do with God's willingness or His ability. Likewise, it also has nothing to do with people not having enough faith. Rather, it is wrapped up in what we actually believe is possible for our lives and what can be released through the church. Our faith will only extend as far as our hope does. If we do not hope for Heaven on earth, we will never actively exercise our faith to bring God's solutions from His world to this one. Oh, but if our hearts taste the hope and the possibility of Heaven on earth, I have good news for you—you quickly become ruined for mediocre Christianity!

POINT OF BREAKTHROUGH

The same God who is able to do anything is also willing to move on our behalf. We are to shake off the deceptions that try to keep us from believing in the willingness of God. Jesus' blood has made us worthy to receive from Heaven's endless supply. God gave us a clear blueprint for what He wills through both Jesus' example and Heaven's culture. This is the model we follow as we discover how to put our faith to action.

RECOMMENDED READING

God Is Not Mad at You by Joyce Meyer

Why Is God So Mad at Me? by Pat Schatzline

When Heaven Invades Earth by Bill Johnson

Hope—The Faith Foundation

~

Now faith is the substance of things hoped for, the evidence of things not seen. —HEBREWS 11:1 KJV

11

How Does Hope Work?

~~

But I will hope continually, and will praise
You yet more and more. —Psalm 71:14

In this section I want to help you upgrade your understanding of what hope is, what it looks like, and how it works in your life. Hope is one of the most ambiguous words in the English language. I am amazed at how many different ways the term is used and applied, particularly among Christians! For most people, hope is a mere wish. In other words, "I hope that I might…" People hope to meet their Mr. or Mrs. Right. People hope to win the lottery. People hope to become successful in their careers. People hope that there will be good boating weather in the morning. People hope to strike it big in Vegas. This version of hope does carry an expectation but, unfortunately, the expectation leans toward the possibility of a desire "not happening."

The most dangerous thing about the contemporary approach to hope is the flightiness and uncertainty associated with it. There is no confidence in the world's definition of hope. In fact, the underlying message seems to be, "Don't get your hopes up!" For many people, hope is a wish that gazes across a bridgeless gulf, daydreaming about the amazing reality that is on the other side—a reality that is completely out of reach unless some type of coincidence happens, our "boat comes in," and "lady luck" pays us a visit. How depressing is that!

Supernatural hope is not idle. Hope that ultimately produces faith is not wishing upon a star. Hope exposes us to realities that are across the gulf and empowers us to actually possess them through using our faith. What is the gulf?

- This gulf is circumstance.

- This gulf is impossibility.

- This gulf is terminal, inoperable, and signed by the doctor.

- This gulf says "no way."

- This gulf says "not a chance."

- This gulf says that restoration is impossible.

- This gulf says "we'll never have that."

- This gulf says our children will never burn passionately for Jesus.

- This gulf says that torment and bondage should just be accepted as a way of life.

Hope is on one side while the object of desire is standing and waiting on the other—and yes, there is an ominous, bridgeless gulf that stands between the two. What we possess by faith that the world does *not have* is the ability to bridge this chasm between where we currently are and what we desire—the object on the other side.

Supernatural hope is not idle.

Hope looks across the gulf of impossibility, sets its gaze upon the promises of God's Word, and supernaturally brings the promises of Scripture into your possession. This is the kind of hope I want us to study and stir up in the chapters ahead!

HOPE IS BIRTHED IN THE LIVING WORD OF GOD

One of the clearest ways we are introduced to hope is through the Person of Jesus Christ—*the* Word of God veiled in flesh. Hope is *not* naming and claiming whatever we want from God. I am not talking about believing God for Armani suits, Bentleys, bigger houses, and all of that stuff. One preacher I heard was shamelessly promoting a series called How to Get Whatever You Need or Desire From God. The principles that I am discussing in this book do not give us license to visualize *whatever* we want, confess it twenty times a day, claim it like we have it, and then tap our foot, expecting God to deliver the goods like He is our cosmic butler. That perspective is hostile to the advancement of the Gospel and to a true, authentic demonstration of supernatural Christianity. It is perverse, unacceptable, and intolerable. In short, it is the devil's counterfeit to what we are talking about here, so just be warned that it is out there.

In the world, objects of "desire" are all across the board, ranging from money to romance to power to fame to pleasure. Even still, these objects remain undefined and unspecified. They are feelings, for sure. People think they know what they are seeking—thrills, pleasure, or security—but ultimately this is the devil's great plan to snare unbelieving humanity. He tries to keep them trapped in a cycle of searching for something without definition. And the results? A people who die Christless and purposeless, squandering both their temporary and eternal lives. The enemy's goal is the same for both believers and unbelievers alike—keep our eyes off the true solution for every void, gulf, and chasm in life—Jesus Christ. For unbelievers, there is a void within their hearts, and the only One capable of satisfying the cry of this deep place is God Himself.

> One of the clearest ways we are introduced
> to hope is through the Person of Jesus
> Christ—*the* Word of God veiled in flesh.

Psalm 42:7 reminds us, *"Deep calls unto deep at the noise of Your waterfalls; all Your waves and billows have gone over me."* The deep of humanity was created to be satisfied by *only* the deep of God's Spirit. The problem is sin. Sin keeps people blind and bound. And yet, sin does not remove the deep void within the core of every person. Satan exploits this, leading people by the leash to every form of "pleasure" imaginable, only to leave them hanging and wanting more at the end.

As believers we have received a very clear vision of legal *objects of desire.* In fact, they could all be summed up in one Person—Jesus Christ. He is called the Desire of Nations (see Haggai 2:7), and rightly so. He is the One capable of not only filling the gulf that aches within every lost human being, but Jesus is the only solution for every single situation, circumstance, and impossibility that we face in our everyday lives. He is the living personification of hope.

Do you want to know what is scripturally legal for you to pray for? Command? Expect? Release? Bind? Loose? Then we need to look at and listen to Jesus Christ.

HOPE EXPOSES US TO KINGDOM REALITIES THAT WERE OFF OUR RADARS

Modern Christians are struggling and dealing with more impossibilities than should be legal. In fact, it is downright illegal for believers to personally experience impossibilities or stand around, witnessing the lives of others being riddled with hopeless situations and circumstances. For those of you uncomfortable with the realities I am presenting here, I want to encourage you to upgrade your definition of hope. This is not Larry Sparks's fantasyland vision of Christianity—it is Jesus' Kingdom-advancing commission.

Are you experiencing any of the gulfs I listed earlier in this chapter in your life? Do you know someone going through an impossible situation? Perhaps they are dealing with sickness or some form of torment or addiction or crumbling family situation. The list of human ills is lengthy, for sure. That said, the list of divine resources that Jesus made available for us to pull from His world into this one is quite lengthy as well.

Do you want to know why many believers who have the supernatural resources of Heaven at their disposal do not access this inheritance? It is because of deception. The devil is in the blinding business (see 2 Cor. 4:4), and he does not stop once we become believers. In the same way that he blinds the minds of unbelievers from being exposed to the *hope* in the Gospel, and ultimately, believing the Good News of Jesus Christ, the same serpent continues to blind the minds of believers from being exposed to the supernatural demonstrations of *hope* presented throughout the Word of God.

Such simple demonstrations of hope are listed right there in Jesus' Christianity 101 lesson to the disciples: *"And as you go, preach, saying, 'The kingdom of heaven is at hand.' Heal the sick, cleanse the lepers, raise the dead, cast out demons. Freely you have received, freely give"* (Matt. 10:7-8). And in Luke 10:1-2, 8-9, we read:

> *After these things the Lord appointed seventy others also, and sent them two by two before His face into every city and place where He Himself was about to go. Then He said to them…"Whatever city you enter, and they receive you, eat such things as are set before you. And heal the sick there, and say to them, 'The kingdom of God has come near to you.'"*

When the disciples, be it the original twelve or the seventy others, were given these instructions from Jesus, the realities that He called them to enforce were, most likely, off their spiritual grids. Heal the sick? Raise the dead? Cast out demons? This was the stuff prophets of old did. Miracles of this caliber were reserved for the venerated, trailblazing forefathers of the faith. And yet, Jesus was releasing a sneak preview to the disciples of what would become available to *every* single believer who was filled with the Holy Spirit. I have to think they were beyond thrilled when they heard this—perhaps even shocked when they actually put these things into practice and witnessed supernatural results!

We see this evidenced when Jesus sent out the seventy and they returned absolutely astounded that the demons were subject to the authority of Jesus' name (see Luke 10:18-20). The point? What Jesus considered to be basic Kingdom protocol has sadly become controversial, fringe, and weird. Again, this is the result of the enemy blinding entire denominations and doctrinal systems to the power of the true Gospel of Jesus Christ.

We need to stop taking our cues from a church, denominational paradigm, doctrine, theology book, celebrity preacher, or pop Christianity, and once again allow Jesus to set our hope level. We hope for what is possible, correct? Jesus exposes us to what is possible, verse after verse, chapter after chapter, throughout the Gospels.

Jesus was releasing a sneak preview to the disciples of what would become available to *every* single believer who was filled with the Holy Spirit.

POINT OF BREAKTHROUGH

Both the example of Jesus and the realities listed throughout the Scripture expose us to new, supernatural possibilities that might have been off our "belief grids." This is the foundation for hope, because hope positions us to recognize that the impossible is now available and accessible to us.

12

THE SUPERNATURAL
POSSIBILITIES OF HOPE

~~

*"God's kingdom" and the "kingdom of heaven" mean
the same thing: the sovereign rule of God (that is,
the rule of heaven, of the one who lives in heaven),
which according to Jesus was and is breaking into
the present world—to earth.* —N.T. WRIGHT[31]

The Spirit of God living within us makes it possible for us to advance the Kingdom wherever we go. This is possible because the powerful Presence of God that is released through our lives actually demonstrates and establishes the Kingdom of God. Pastor and author Tullian Tchividjian writes, "Christians are called to follow Jesus, to go where He's going and to do what He's doing."[32] This is the essence of advancing the Kingdom of God. So what does this look like? Jesus sums it up in Matthew 10:8, when He instructs the disciples to *"heal the sick, cleanse the lepers, raise the dead, cast out demons. Freely you have received, freely give."*

The Kingdom of Heaven Is At Hand

The Kingdom of God is a present-tense reality, not simply a future-tense expectation. Jesus specifically explains in Luke 17:20-21, *"The kingdom of God does not come with observation; nor will they say, 'See here!' or 'See there!' For indeed, the kingdom of God is within you."* Jesus made it clear that the Kingdom is not something we are waiting on—it is already present with power. We should not place restriction on how much of the Kingdom we are able to experience and enjoy now, this side of eternity. Dallas Willard notes that "what we are aiming for in this vision is to live fully in the Kingdom of God and as fully as possible now and here, not just hereafter."[33]

One of the fundamental things that hope does is expose us to different Kingdom realities that were previously off our spiritual grids and stirs us to relentlessly pursue these realities to be released in our lives. In the following pages, we will explore some of the "common" truths that should be on *all* of our spiritual grids and part of our everyday Christian lives.

The Spirit of God living within us makes it possible for us to advance the Kingdom wherever we go.

Heal the Sick

Then Jesus went about all the cities and villages, teaching in their synagogues, preaching the gospel of the kingdom, and healing every sickness and every disease among the people (Matthew 9:35).

God wills to heal, not because He simply wants to enhance our comfort on earth—He desires, wills, and, yes, even delights to heal because it is a sign of the in-breaking rule and reign of His Kingdom. Supernatural healing is frequently listed side by side with the Gospel of the Kingdom. Just as salvation restores God's original intent of humanity being able to walk in fellowship with Him, healing miracles do likewise.

The devil would like nothing more than for us to throw out the proverbial baby with the bathwater. Healing is not a doctrine; it's not even part of the Gospel. Tim Keller comments, "We modern people think of miracles as the suspension of the natural order, but Jesus meant them to be the restoration of the natural order."[34] Remember, the model of Jesus and the culture of Heaven are our blueprints when it comes to defining God's will. When healing happens, God's original intent is being released into a present-day situation or circumstance. Wholeness is Heaven's agenda.

So many Christians shrug off the topic of supernatural healing because of imbalance, misuse, abuse, or bad—*really* bad—theology. If this is you, then I can truly sympathize as I have been exposed to so-called healing ministries that were nothing more than smoke and mirrors intended to stir excitement in order to empty wallets. Regardless of the negative impressions you may have received about divine healing, signs, wonders, and miracles, it is wise to embrace a fresh perspective on the subject and expose yourself to the possibility of healing once again.

Healing demonstrates the supremacy of Jesus Christ over all things. Additionally, signs, wonders, and healing miracles reveal the glory of God. Evangelist Randy Clark notes, "The Bible contains eighteen categories of instances where the glory of God is mentioned. By far, the largest category is miracles and healings, where God's glory is connected thirty times to a demonstration of His power through the working of signs, wonders and miracles."[35]

When disease and sickness is overcome by the powerful Presence of God, the exclusive authority in Jesus' name is made known to every on-looker and observer. No, healing miracles do *not* guarantee conversions. However, the miraculous has historically opened the door for tremendous evangelism opportunities.

In summary, Jesus healed *all* who came to Him (see Matt. 4:23). Jesus modeled this lifestyle during His three-plus years of public ministry, and then passed the baton when He sent us out just as He was sent. Healing the sick is part of the Great Commission and is a sign that should follow every believer (see Mark 16:17-18); and James gives instructions for the elders for pray for the sick (see James 5:13-15). Miracles and the gift of healings are two of the nine gifts of the Holy Spirit that are sovereignly distributed to believers as the Holy Spirit wills—and they should be desired and expected *today* (see 1 Cor. 12:9-11).[36] I pray that hope arises in your spirit that supernatural healing is not only possible but available to you and *through* you to others.

> **Healing demonstrates the supremacy**
> **of Jesus over all things.**

CLEANSE THE LEPERS

Tell them that the kingdom is here. Bring health to the sick. Raise the dead. Touch the untouchables. Kick out demons. You have been treated generously, so live generously (Matthew 10:8 MSG).

There are many people who are under the assumption that they are unclean and unfit, not merely for church attendance, but for God's acceptance. What is Jesus' response to this? He touched them, completely transforming their very identity. They went from being untouchable to touched by the Most Holy. We have been commissioned and empowered to release that same transformative touch of Jesus *today*.

While we do not confront physical leprosy too much today, we still deal with those who have been written off as unclean and unworthy. I remember hearing a statement from a guy who had a "church history," but was intimidated at setting foot inside a church today for fear of what might happen—as if the church would not be able to handle his uncleanness and sin, and the walls would cave in. This absolutely broke my heart and stirred up a little righteous indignation within. For someone to actually believe such a deception reflects poorly upon church culture. We cannot disregard the reality of our Savior who fearlessly touched the unclean and revealed the Father's heart of love and compassion toward the outcast.

Unfortunately, the church seems to be afraid of the world's uncleanness contaminating us. If we continue preaching a message of separatism, calling believers to isolate themselves from the world for fear of the world rubbing off on us, our vision of the indwelling power and Presence of God within us becomes perverted—big time. To model Jesus is to embrace the criticism and persecution that Jesus experienced. He was ridiculed by the religious people time after time for touching those who were unclean and unworthy (by the religious people's standards). And yet, the Man Christ Jesus was so full of the Holy Spirit's Presence and power that there was no thought as to whether or not the leprosy would "rub off on Him" and contaminate His perfection.

Under the Old Covenant system, contamination was real. If someone touched something unclean, they would become contaminated. But now we have the Presence of the Holy Spirit dwelling within us, empowering us to touch the unclean and "unworthy" with the transformative love, power, and compassion of King Jesus. Jesus' touch did not subject Him to contamination. Quite the opposite, in fact—His touch gloriously "contaminated" the unclean with the identity and love of Heaven.

Your touch is your love, your genuine friendship, your encouragement, and your presence. People are not evangelism projects meant to be "saved." Those who do not know Jesus are orphans who need to be united with the Father. We do not befriend people *just* to evangelize them; we befriend and love them because they are valuable to God. He created every single human being in His image. They are loved, cherished, and full of history-making potential.

One of the great historical figures who modeled Jesus' cleansing touch was evangelist and healing minister John G. Lake. There is an incredible testimony of Lake being so bold in the midst of the bubonic plague outbreak that he had some of the plague-ridden foam from a corpse placed onto his hand. Under a microscope, it was revealed that Lake was not the one contaminated; it was actually the germs that ended up dying instantly because of Lake's touch. This illustrates the power of what and Who we offer every single person who is plagued by sin, hopelessness, condemnation, and lies about his or her "unclean" identity. Our touch unveils a God who longs to reach out to every single person on the planet with the love and compassion of Jesus Christ.

> **Now we have the Presence of the Holy Spirit dwelling within us, empowering us to touch the unclean and "unworthy" with the transformative love, power, and compassion of King Jesus.**

RAISE THE DEAD

Heal the sick, cleanse the lepers, raise the dead… (Matthew 10:8).

Jesus raised the dead because of the anointing, or indwelling Presence of the Holy Spirit, that was within Him. The same Jesus made it clear that you and I can accomplish this same supernatural act by the same supernatural Spirit who resides within each of us.

It happened in the Old Testament, it was there in the Gospels, and yes, it also took place through the disciples in the Book of Acts. It may seem crazy, outlandish, and infrequent in our modern Western Christian culture, but it is nevertheless something that we have received the capacity to release because of the anointing on our lives.

The Holy Spirit wants to upgrade our hope—just because we do not see something happening in our country, in our own backyard, does not mean it is an invalid experience that we should not contend for. If anything, the lack of what we see should drive us into the Word of God, not satisfied with where we are, and cause us to cry out in hunger to see and release the impossible realms of the Kingdom of Heaven into the earth. It is possible and it is available for us today.

In the Old Testament, we read of Elijah and Elisha raising people from the dead. This would make sense; after all, these men were powerfully anointed prophets of God. Even after Elisha was dead and gone, his very bones raised a man from the dead (2 Kings 13:20-21)!

Each of us has received something *greater* than Elisha. Elisha's bones were not special; it was what they were exposed to that charged them with supernatural healing power, and that was the Presence and power of God. He received a double portion of Elijah's anointing, and, as a result, Elisha was so possessed by God that even after his physical death, his body was still miraculously brimming with power because of the Holy Spirit's resting upon Him. And yet, each one of us has what Elijah and Elisha did not: Christ *in* you, which is the hope of glory (see Col. 1:27).

We know that Jesus raised people from the dead, but then again, *that was Jesus.* We must change our perspective concerning this issue. Jesus raised the dead through the power of the Holy Spirit, something that was transferable. In Matthew 10:8 Jesus told the disciples, *"Freely you have received...."* This is significant because Jesus was revealing that the power to raise the dead was not locked up in His divinity and unavailable to all normal people. To the twelve disciples, and later to the seventy, this power and authority was transferred for a season. For you and me it was transferred with permanence because of the coming of the Spirit on Pentecost. The Spirit who raises the dead now lives inside of you and me!

What is the key to unlocking and releasing this power? It begins with having hope for the possibility. Once we remove "raising the dead" from the category of exploits reserved for the spiritual history-makers or powerfully anointed Bible characters of old, and start believing it is available for us today, we will start to witness an increase in people being raised from the dead.

It has little to do with putting some formula into practice and a lot to do with simple hope. Do we believe that raising the dead is even possible today? Once the body of Christ hopes in this reality again, we position ourselves to start releasing it through faith. Faith will only pull into reality what we believe is possible.

The Spirit who raises the dead now lives inside of you!

CAST OUT DEMONS

How God anointed Jesus of Nazareth with the Holy Spirit and with power, who went about doing good and healing all who were oppressed by the devil, for God was with Him (Acts 10:38).

Remember, the same Holy Spirit who anointed Jesus of Nazareth with the power to heal *all* who were oppressed by the devil, and the same Spirit who empowered the early Christians to practice exorcism as normal, everyday life, also lives inside of us. Dr. Graham Twelftree brings a scripturally sound, academic perspective to the normalcy of casting out demons, observing that "just as Jesus had authority to perform exorcisms and to heal, and as the apostles received authority over demons, authority to defeat Satan, so the early Christians had been given that authority to be involved in the same preliminary defeat of Satan."[37] Satan has already been defeated because of the cross of Christ, but the world still suffers under his tyranny. You and I are the ones empowered to enforce Jesus' finished work and secured victory over every part of the planet that has been infected by darkness.

The "normal" ministry of casting out demons is one of the most misunderstood topics in the body of Christ today. This must become normal—not weird, bizarre, or reserved for a dark, back room—otherwise it will continue to remain mystified, and, as a result, continue to go undone. Casting out demons, or deliverance ministry, is absolutely integral to advancing God's Kingdom and preaching the full Gospel message. Francis MacNutt writes, "Only when we are able to free the oppressed and heal those suffering from the curse of sickness can we really preach Christ's basic message: The Kingdom of God is at hand and the kingdom of Satan is being destroyed."[38]

Deliverance from demonic oppression has little to do with some spectacle that takes place during prayer. We expect a scene out of *The Exorcist* and, in turn, withdraw from this vital ministry. As a result, so many people have remained in torment and bondage to the powers of darkness. It is important that during deliverance we do not focus on the fanfare—bodies contorting, eyes rolling back, demonic voices—but we focus on releasing freedom to the individual who has been tormented.

Fanfare does not equal freedom. Will unusual things happen? Of course they will. Kris Vallotton explains, "People experience many different kinds of manifestations when they are getting free. You cannot measure the level of someone's freedom by the amount of drama a demon displays in exiting. In fact, the most freedom is usually experienced with the least amount of deliverance drama."[39]

> **You and I are the ones empowered to enforce Jesus' finished work and secured victory over every part of the planet that has been impacted by darkness.**

FREELY RECEIVE, FREELY GIVE

The process of unlocking a supernatural culture in the church starts with a widespread acknowledgement of hope in the present-day power of the Kingdom. If we do not even believe that these Kingdom exploits are accessible and available for us today, we will never possess the hope that leads to faith.

Prayer leader Corey Russell says, "Revival is not out with the old and in with the new. Revival is out with the old, and in with the even older."[40] The reason why revival in a contemporary context is often associated with signs, wonders, and supernatural phenomena is because to revive authentic New Testament Christianity, there must be a simultaneous resurgence of the supernatural. This is what the early church moved in as the normal expression of faith. It was not weird; it was completely normal. In fact, what we consider weird today is what would have been considered normal back then. It would have been weird for the New Testament church *not* to have seen people healed from sickness, delivered from demonic oppression, and, yes, raised from the dead on a regular basis.

Jesus made a significant example for us when He demonstrated how the power He walked in was transferable to everyday people. First, the twelve disciples, then the seventy, and finally, every single believer became eligible for this power transfer after the Holy Spirit was poured out at Pentecost.

> **The process of unlocking a supernatural culture in the church starts with a widespread acknowledgement of hope in the present-day power of the Kingdom.**

The truth is that because we have greatly received, we, in turn, have the spiritual capacity to powerfully give. We have received the very Spirit of God. Because of this, we have become positioned to become catalysts to giving away the very Presence and power that we received. How do we give it away? We just explored some of the key methods that are often overlooked, and yet, they are the very methods that Jesus demonstrated the most—healing the sick, casting out demons, touching the untouchable, and raising the dead.

POINT OF BREAKTHROUGH

For us to walk in the present-day power of the Kingdom of God, it is vital that we look back to the ministry of Jesus Christ and study the works He did. This is what the early church modeled, and this is what normal Christianity should look like today. Powerlessness is not the result of a lack of faith; it is the result of not having hope for the availability and accessibility of the supernatural in our lives and churches today.

RECOMMENDED READING

Taking Action by Reinhard Bonnke

Gifts of the Spirit by Derek Prince

Unfashionable by Tullian Tchividjian

Spirit Wars by Kris Vallotton

Deliverance From Evil Spirits by Francis MacNutt

The Nearly Perfect Crime by Francis MacNutt

Raising the Dead by Chauncey Crandall, MD

13

HOPE CONFRONTS AND CHANGES THE IMPOSSIBLE

～～

Faith is the confidence that what we hope for
will actually happen; it gives us assurance about
things we cannot see. —HEBREWS 11:1 NLT

Hope sees something in the unseen, holds onto it, and will not let it go until that unseen promise becomes a visible reality. We press in until the impossible becomes possible and the circumstance is supernaturally turned around. Hope is far more wild and radical than mere belief. Hope is consumed by a possibility and will not back down or let go until that possibility becomes a reality. Hope confronts us with new possibility; faith turns that possibility into reality through the power of God.

Hope is the most wonderful prison that we could be locked up in. Zechariah 9:12 actually uses the phrase, *"prisoners of hope."* Just like prison cells hold people captive, hope is a cell that imprisons us to what is possible in the realms of God. We are imprisoned to the idea of something that is currently not a reality *becoming* a reality. Those imprisoned by hope have no choice but to activate breakthrough faith. They are totally consumed by the drive to see the supernatural promises of Scripture transform every impossible, hopeless situation they face.

> Hope confronts us with new possibility; faith turns
> that possibility into reality through the power of God.

FAITH IS THE SUBSTANCE OF HOPE

Now faith is the substance of things hoped for, the evidence of things not seen. For by it the elders obtained a good testimony (Hebrews 11:1-2).

When we know what to do with hope, we are then able to activate our faith. It is faith that produces measurable results. Hope is essential; but remember that it is a foundation and catalyst to faith. We cannot arrive at hope and stop there. Hope was never intended to be separate from faith, for it is the absolutely necessary foundation. Faith and hope are parts of an essential spiritual equation that we need to understand in order to see possibilities become realities in our life.

Maybe some of the things that we have discussed so far are off your spiritual grid. Maybe you didn't think God that did this kind of thing anymore—healing the sick, casting out demons, or raising the dead. Nevertheless, you are convinced that the same God who is able to speak planets into orbit is the very God who is able and willing to bring your situation into divine alignment with the blueprint of His Word and His Kingdom.

You are full of hope. God said it and you believe it. You are gripped with realities in Scripture and you cannot shake them. You see Jesus commanding impossibilities to bow before Him continually, and you recognize that through the Great Commission you too have been empowered to see impossibilities shift and produce Christ-exalting miracles. You are not commanding God; you are enforcing His will on the earth as a member of the Matthew 16 church—the one that binds what is already bound in Heaven and releases that which is normal in Heaven.

Once we know that God is able *and* willing to do what He said and what is outlined in His Word, then we can begin introducing ourselves to truth after truth and reality after reality of what God wants to do in and through our lives. When these truths and realities are settled in our spirits, we have all of the elements in place that we need to activate faith.

OUR FORERUNNER AND EXAMPLE OF HOPE: ABRAHAM

The Word of the Lord Introduces Hope

God's interaction with Abram (AKA: Abraham) is a prophetic picture of His interactions with you and me. What is the secret to introducing realities that confront the impossibilities of life? The word of the Lord.

> *After these things the word of the Lord came to Abram in a vision, saying, "Do not be afraid, Abram. I am your shield, your exceedingly great reward." But Abram said, "Lord God, what will You give me, seeing I go childless, and the heir of my house is Eliezer of Damascus?" Then Abram said, "Look, You have given me no offspring; indeed one born in my house is my heir!" And behold, the word of the Lord came to him, saying, "This one shall not be your heir, but one who will come from your own body shall be your heir"* (Genesis 15:1-4).

Verse 4 is where God introduces the possibility that was previously off of Abram's spiritual grid: he was actually going to have a child from his own body. Abram and his wife were both well beyond hope at the time. He was too old and Sarai's womb was too barren. They had a lot going against them. Maybe this is where you are at right now, or maybe you cannot bear to watch countless lives continue to crumble beneath the hopeless situations plaguing them.

Abram's hope for the impossible becoming possible was born when the word of the Lord came to Abram. We too have the Word of God. That precious book called the Bible is filled with promises that confront hopelessness, impossibility, and every single situation or circumstance that threatens to come against us.

HOPE TRANSFORMS HOW WE RESPOND TO THE WORD OF THE LORD

Abram (now Abraham) so internalized the hope-stirring Word of God that he was able to stare hopelessness in the face...and believe God *anyway*. He believed God despite the circumstances he was up against. Paul draws some powerful implications from the life of Abraham.

> *Therefore it is of faith that it might be according to grace, so that the promise might be sure to all the seed, not only to those who are of the law, but also to those who are of the faith of Abraham, who is the father of us all (as it is written, "I have made you a father of many nations") in the presence of Him whom he believed—God, who gives life to the dead and calls those things which do not exist as though they did; who, contrary to hope, in hope believed, so that he became the father of many nations, according to what was spoken, "So shall your descendants be." And not being weak in faith, he did not consider his own body, already dead (since he was about a hundred years old), and the deadness of Sarah's womb* (Romans 4:16-21).

The promise finally came to fruition and Abraham became the father of many nations. What did Abraham do with the word of the Lord that he received? It was more than reading it. It was more than just hearing it. It was more than thinking about it, confessing it, claiming it, and naming it. He stood on it relentlessly and refused to budge—it was his steady anchor during difficult times.

Hope Is Anchored in God's Unchanging, Eternal Character

What kept Abraham from wavering and what was his source of strength during this time? It was God alone. Paul goes on to say:

> *He did not waver at the promise of God through unbelief, but was strengthened in faith, giving glory to God, and being fully convinced that what He had promised He was also able to perform* (Romans 4:20-21).

All we need to know is who God is and leave the execution of the impossible up to Him. He is healer. He is deliverer. He is redeemer. He is provider. He is restorer. He is Creator. These titles are not up for debate. Our hope is birthed in the knowledge of who God is, so when we internalize a promise from His Word, it is not just thinking happy thoughts or naming and claiming something; rather, our souls actually become anchored in an unchangeable, unshakeable reality that is rooted in the very name and nature of God almighty. This births a prevailing hope—a hope like Abraham's that, after some trial and error, stared impossibilities in the face and revealed the supernatural source of this hope. Read the last verse. Abraham was *"fully convinced that what He had promised He was also able to perform."* The God who made Abraham an impossible-sounding promise was also faithful to deliver on what He said. This God has *not* changed for you or me today.

YOU'RE IN ON IT

Just as God exposed Abraham to possibilities that were off his grid and gave him supernatural hope to believe for the impossible, God wants to do the same thing for each of us *today*. The Message Bible puts Acts 10:34 this way: *"God plays no favorites!"* If God worked the miraculous for Abraham thousands of years ago, then He will surely be faithful to do it again for us today!

Abraham was a prophetic model for you and me, as he was recognized as the first person on the planet to "walk by faith." In Romans 4 Paul identified Abraham as the "father" of our faith in God. He was not considered righteous because of his good works, but because of his faith. In the same way you and I are not given right standing with God because of anything we have done or could do, but because of what Jesus Christ did on the cross on our behalf.

Our hope is birthed in the knowledge of who God is.

We are now ready to start exploring the dynamics of faith. So many people want to jump right into the *hows of faith* without knowing the *who of faith*. As a result, we end up using faith as a spiritual tool to bring about our own selfish desires and wants. Faith is truly a blank check, but it will not function properly if put in the hands of someone who perverts it for personal gain. A lifestyle of breakthrough faith is not reserved for the perfect; it is, however, available to those who will steward it well for the glory of God.

In the pages to come we are going to discover how to put this spiritual blank check to work and actually experience the supernatural results God has always intended for His people to walk in. I will also be sharing more of my personal journey into this lifestyle of faith. As someone who has experienced the faith imbalance on both sides—people who used it for personal gain and people who underused it because of a skewed perspective of humility—God has given me some transferable lessons that will empower each of us to activate authentic breakthrough faith in our lives.

POINT OF BREAKTHROUGH

Abram is a powerful example of how hope works for us today. Even though circumstances were against him and the promise of God's Word sounded impossible, Abram recognized that the One who made the promise was both supernatural and faithful. Though he made mistakes, Abram persevered and believed God. As a result, hope released faith that brought forth his miracle son, Isaac. Hope is the birthplace for the impossible to happen in our lives. If God performed the miraculous for Abraham, then He can and will do it for us because He plays no favorites.

Part Two

~~~

ACTIVATING BREAKTHROUGH FAITH

DEVELOP

~

*And again He entered Capernaum after some days, and
it was heard that He was in the house. Immediately
many gathered together, so that there was no longer
room to receive them, not even near the door. And He
preached the word to them. Then they came to Him,
bringing a paralytic who was carried by four men.
And when they could not come near Him because of
the crowd, they uncovered the roof where He was. So
when they had broken through, they let down the bed
on which the paralytic was lying. —*MARK 2:1-4

We have been laying the necessary groundwork to understanding
breakthrough faith. Now we will practically discover what this
breakthrough faith actually looks like, how it functions in our lives,
and some of the ways we can start living out this supernatural lifestyle.
In the next several chapters, we will study the account of the paralytic
man from Mark 2. This account gives us an incredible example of what
it looks like to both release and sustain breakthrough faith.

So here is the question: Are we going to fold beneath our circumstances, or are we going to believe that the almighty God who lives

inside of us can and will miraculously *transform* our circumstances? If He already lives within us, then we do not have to muster up faith; as we will soon discover, we have actually received God's own faith!

This truth gives us the ability to model the faith of the paralytic's friends who were so confident in the character of Jesus, so expectant that this Jesus was both able and willing to heal, and so fueled up on hope, that their only option was breaking through a ceiling to get to this Jesus and *experience* His perfect will.

Too many Christians are up, down, left, and right. They taste seasonal victory and then celebrate. No sooner after they experience breakthrough in one area they find themselves struggling in another. Jesus was not kidding about what we would experience in this life. He said, *"In the world you will have tribulation; but be of good cheer, I have overcome the world"* (John 16:33).

Life *will* happen. The worst type of "faith theology" we can possibly buy into is that "if you have enough faith" or make "the right confessions" or "pray the right prayers" or "give money to a church or ministry," you will never experience opposition or resistance. I have experienced this perspective firsthand, and I will candidly share some of my personal testimony on how I navigated through the counterfeit in order to begin walking in breakthrough faith.

So what's the balance? While Jesus said that tribulation would come, He also gave us a glimpse of the supernatural inheritance that every believer is licensed to walk in. Circumstances will come, but we do not face them as a powerless people; we face them in Christ, and with Christ living on the inside of us. The One who, according to John 16:33, *"deprived it* (the world) *of power to harm you and has conquered it for you,"* (AMP) has made you His dwelling place. If Jesus is victorious, then you too get to partake in His victory.

If you are currently facing something that is obviously not God's will (either for your life or for someone else's), I pray that a holy tenacity starts rising up within you that burns to break through whatever barriers you are facing and apprehend God's promises through faith. Hope exposed you to some powerful new possibilities; now, it is time for you to see these possibilities become your new reality!

Circumstances will come, but we do not face them as a powerless people; we face them in Christ, and with Christ living on the inside of us.

14

FAITH 101

~~

For by grace you have been saved through faith, and that
not of yourselves; it is the gift of God. —EPHESIANS 2:8

While there is undeniable mystery attached to the sovereign Creator of all things, there are several subjects that both the Word of God and the example of Jesus give clear instructions on how to deal with. We identified a few of these topics in our section on the supernatural power of the Kingdom. And here we will identify a few others.

We know that God has a will. We also know the devil has a will. This means that we cannot just accept what life throws our way as God's will because all too often we embrace the assault of the devil and mistakenly label it as God's doing. This is a travesty that must be confronted. Remember, the paralytic's friends did not idly accept their friend's circumstances as God's will. No. They had a clear vision of God's will as revealed through the example of Jesus, which was shared with them through testimony. They heard that Jesus was a Miracle Worker and that no diseased, afflicted, tormented people were turned away from His Presence.

As a result of what they knew about Jesus, they *pressed through* the boundaries and roadblocks to purposefully step into God's will. So many of us are under the false assumption that God's will just happens. It does not. He has revealed His will through the written Word and through the model of Jesus Christ. Ask the Holy Spirit to come and give you understanding, discernment, and clarity concerning the revolutionary biblical concepts we are about to study.

WHERE DOES FAITH COME FROM?

Faith is not something that we just come up with in our own ability; we received faith as a gift from a gracious God the day we were translated out of darkness into the Kingdom of God and were born again. Each of us received breakthrough faith the day we became a believer in the Lord Jesus Christ! Ephesians 2:8-9 gives us the clearest picture of how we received faith for salvation: *"For by grace you have been saved through faith. And this is not your own doing; it is the gift of God, not a result of works, so that no one may boast"* (ESV).

Faith does not come from us. It is not natural in origin. As human beings, we do not have the ability to just conjure up faith. The first activation of faith that we make is when we trust in the finished work of Jesus on the cross. To believe the message of the Gospel and actually become transformed by it demands supernatural faith. This is why so many mock the message of the cross.

Paul was absolutely correct in remarking that *"the message of the cross is foolishness to those who are perishing"* (1 Cor. 1:18). This verse alone refutes the idea that we can will up enough faith to become a Christian. Apart from God's invasion, the Gospel remains foolish. You and I are perishing *until* God supernaturally confronts us and miraculously deposits faith into our spirits. It takes a miraculous act of God for us to believe in the message of the cross. Apart from God giving each of us the "measure of faith," it is absolutely impossible for us to embrace the liberating truth of salvation and become born again.

Here is the problem then: when we view faith as something we can create on our own, then we will always be striving toward an upgrade, a new level, or a fresh revelation in order to receive more faith. There will always be *more* faith that we can possess, earn, attain, or build.

In Ephesians 2:8-9 Paul is very intentional about reminding us that faith is nothing we can will up using our own strength or willpower. Faith to believe in God's grace is a wondrous gift of God. Faith is a gift and grace is a gift. We cannot earn salvation. We cannot work for it. We cannot do enough good things to include ourselves in God's family, and there are not too many bad things we can do to exclude us. God gives you and me supernatural faith to believe in His unmerited, amazing grace. Billy Graham describes faith as "the channel through which God's grace to us is received. It is the hand that reaches out and receives the gift of His love."[41]

**Each of us received *breakthrough faith* the day
we became a believer in the Lord Jesus Christ!**

The process is completely supernatural, through and through. The Spirit of God is the One who comes and plants this faith within us. It is this supernatural faith that empowers us to believe the most wild and outstanding story ever told—the story of the Gospel and how the message of a Man, a rugged cross, and an empty tomb can actually bring the spiritually dead to life. And this happens in our day.

WHERE DOES BREAKTHROUGH FAITH COME FROM?

Mark 11:22-23 is the passage that contains the hidden secret to unlocking the breakthrough, miracle-working realm of faith:

> *So Jesus answered and said to them, "Have faith in God. For assuredly, I say to you, whoever says to this mountain, 'Be removed and be cast into the sea,' and does not doubt in his heart, but believes that those things he says will be done, he will have whatever he says."*

First and foremost, we must realize that *there are no categories or levels of faith.* We have received the same faith as the apostle Paul. In fact, according to the most accurate translation of Mark 11:22, we have received the very faith *of* God.

Consider this for a moment: the faith we received at salvation did not come from us; it came from God. If this is true, then it is impossible for us to qualify for a faith upgrade or receive a "new level" of faith. We cannot go higher, deeper, or farther than the faith *of* God. The only thing we can learn how to do more effectively is steward what we have already been given. This is what positions us to walk in increased breakthrough, victory, and miracles.

But what about the often-quoted Romans 10:17 passage: *"So then faith comes by hearing, and hearing by the word of God"*? Many use this passage to imply that we can get *more* faith by spending time reading the Bible or listening to sermons. While those things are definitely beneficial and helpful to our growth, they are incorrect and out of context when applied to this verse. Go to Romans Chapter 10 and read the surrounding verses. Paul is specifically talking about faith for salvation here. Right before verse 17, he asks,

> *How then shall they call on Him in whom they have not believed? And how shall they believe in Him of whom they have not heard? And how shall they hear without a preacher? And how shall they preach unless they are sent? As it is written: "How beautiful are the feet of those who preach the gospel of peace, who bring glad tidings of good things!" But they have not all obeyed the gospel. For Isaiah says, "Lord, who has believed our report?"* (Romans 10:14-16)

Faith to believe the Gospel and become born again comes from God *through* His Word! Does studying Scripture help our faith? Yes. The Word of God is the written record of what faith legally can withdraw from Heaven and release into the earth. Scripture makes us aware of what faith is able to do; however, it does *not* increase the quantity of our faith! Remember, there are no levels of faith. What we received at salvation is completely supernatural and entirely sufficient for everything from saving our souls to raising the dead.

Now for the balance. Even though you have received this seed of faith at the moment of salvation—faith capable of both saving your soul and working the miraculous—*you* have a responsibility to work this faith out on a practical, day-to-day basis. You are the steward of your faith, just like you are the steward of the muscles in your body. Just as it is with your physical muscles, the muscle of faith is within you, waiting to be worked out.

While I do not believe we should spend our time begging God for "more faith," I am thoroughly convinced that we should invest that energy in growing and *developing* our faith. This entire section is a "How-To" guide dedicated to help you exercise your faith through: declaring God's Word, being strengthened by testimony, pursuing God's presence, renewing your mind, and pressing through the obstacles hindering your breakthrough.

Return to the muscle example and now, think of your faith like a spiritual muscle. When you go to the gym, you are not exercising with the intention of literally getting more muscles. You are not lifting weights, thinking that more muscle tissue is going to supernaturally form in your body. The muscle is already there; exercise strengthens it and "works it out."

The phrase "work out" is very appropriate when it comes to faith. Even though you have received a deposit of this mountain-moving faith, there are certain things you must do in order to exercise faith so it can start producing supernatural results in your life. To build muscle you need to exercise. The same is true for faith.

F. F. Bosworth once observed that, "Most Christians feed their body three hot meals a day and their spirit one cold snack a week. And they wonder why they're so weak in faith." I encourage you to make the necessary investments in building your faith. Strengthen the most important muscle you've got. I promise you, the spiritual muscle of faith will trump anything that your natural, physical muscles are capable of.

THE FAITH OF HISTORY MAKERS

Study the lives of those who changed nations, helped shape Christianity over the centuries, and saw multitudes comes to Christ. Those who have been powerfully used by God throughout the ages did not pursue some type of upgraded faith. Rather, they recognized the power of the faith they received at conversion and lived like what they got from God was supernatural and sufficient for the job of changing the world.

Who are your personal heroes of the faith? Maybe it is the audacious reformer Martin Luther. His breakthrough faith compelled him to nail the Ninety-five Theses to the door of the University Church in Wittenberg and incite a spiritual revolution.[42] Maybe it is John Wesley, the founder of Methodism and firebrand evangelist who preached with such anointing and power that "well-dressed, mature people suddenly cried out as if in the agonies of death. Both men and women, outside and inside the church buildings, would tremble and sink to the ground."[43]

Perhaps it is Jonathan Edwards, the theologian, scholar, and preacher who experienced revival in such a dynamic measure that the entire community of Northampton, Massachusetts, was said to be "permeated by divine presence," where "simply upon entering the community, the people's skepticism (about the revival) inevitably dissipated because of the overwhelming presence of God."[44] And I cannot help but think of young Evan Roberts, the catalyst of the great Welsh Revival of 1904, who saw 100,000 souls converted to Christ and an entire region transformed by the power of God. Every one of us possesses the same faith that each of these world changers did!

> **What we received at salvation is completely supernatural and entirely sufficient for everything from saving our souls to raising the dead.**

These are but a few names handpicked from history. In recent years I have reflected on spiritual generals like evangelist Billy Graham. Study his past and you will be amazingly unimpressed. Born on a dairy farm and raised during the Great Depression, the man went on to become a spiritual advisor to presidents and one of the most powerful evangelists of our time. It was said that as a child he was denied membership in a local youth group because he was "too worldly."[45]

Graham was almost thrown out of a Christian college, with the leadership warning him, "At best, all you could amount to would be a poor country Baptist preacher somewhere out in the sticks…. You have a voice that pulls. God can use that voice of yours. He can use it mightily."[46] What happened? Graham stewarded the faith he received and used it to change the world through his evangelistic influence. He faced opposition like all of us do, but he persevered not because he received a super-charged "Billy Graham kind of faith," but because he recognized that the faith he already had was otherworldly and supernatural.

One of my personal heroes was evangelist Kathryn Kuhlman. The woman was as unlikely a candidate as anyone to have a history-making, Spirit-filled miracle ministry. She was a young girl from *nowheresville* in Concordia, Missouri.[47] She lived at a time when women preachers were not as embraced as they are today. She had setbacks, failures, and nearly debilitating odds stacked against her. The result was that she emerged as one of the most powerful evangelists of her day, demonstrating the love and power of the Holy Spirit time after time in her crusades, with multitudes coming to Christ and receiving supernatural healing.

If you listen to or read anything from Kathryn, you will notice how frequently she refers to her new-birth experience. Why? It was at the age of fourteen in her quaint little Methodist church where the seed of breakthrough faith was planted in her heart as she gave her life to Jesus. The very faith that released miracles, signs, and wonders was not because of some special anointing she received later on in life, after having countless people pray for her and visiting every crusade or conference on the planet. Kathryn's approach was simple: she "always preached faith in a big God. Faith in a God big enough to cross any hurdle was a principle she not only preached, but lived by."[48] She learned to steward the faith she received as a little girl.

History makers like these notable individuals stir us up—and then quickly let us down. We assume they possessed some special, upgraded type of faith—the special mountain-moving faith we read about in Mark 11:22-23. But this is not true. What separates heroes and history makers from those who do nothing, living in regret and complaint because they didn't receive "that kind of faith"? Stewardship. Each of us has the same faith as Billy Graham. We all have the miracle-working faith of Kathryn Kuhlman! I pray that you would recognize that the faith you received is capable of accomplishing anything—and everything. It is not yours; it is a gift from a gracious God.

THE FAITH OF GOD

The supernatural faith that saved you is the same faith that releases the power to heal the sick, cast out demons, raise the dead, and, yes, even transform entire nations through the power and Presence of God. Bible teacher Andrew Wommack poignantly settles the "levels of faith" debate by explaining,

> One of the areas about faith that gives people the most trouble is the concept that we have to acquire more faith and that some people have much faith, while others have virtually none. We spend a lot of effort, like a dog chasing its tail, trying to get something we already have. Every born-again Christian already has the same quality and quantity of faith that Jesus has.[49]

In Mark 11:22, when Jesus says *"have faith in God,"* the most accurate translation of this statement is *"have the faith of God."* If the faith we receive at salvation comes *from* God, then it makes sense that we actually receive the faith *of* God. Where does God get the faith that He gives us? *From Himself.* This then begs the question, "Does God have faith?" Look back at Genesis 1 for a moment, where God speaks into nothingness and creates the world. He had faith in His Word, that what He said would come to pass. God has faith, and we become partakers of this same faith through the new-birth experience.

The faith you received is capable of accomplishing anything.

It literally takes the faith of God to be converted to Christianity. If this is indeed true, then we have the very faith of God *living* on the inside of us. It is a *living* faith because it comes from the *living God*. Jesus explained, *"For assuredly, I say to you, if you have faith as a mustard seed, you will say to this mountain, 'Move from here to there,' and it will move; and nothing will be impossible for you"* (Matthew 17:20).

Faith as a mustard seed. This was not Jesus' attempt to categorize levels of faith (some have mustard-seed level faith, some have apple-seed level faith, etc.). Jesus was telling us that because we received the faith of God, even if this faith was the size of a mustard seed, it did not matter because it would produce a God-sized harvest. A mustard seed of faith from us cannot move a hill of beans, but a mustard seed of faith *from God* can move mountains, shake nations, and change the world.

Now that we know where breakthrough faith comes from (God), I want us to continue to study the story of the paralytic in Mark 2 and discover some practical keys on how we can start putting this faith to action.

POINT OF BREAKTHROUGH

Breakthrough faith is not some new level of faith. It is not an upgrade. It is not reserved for extraordinary, unusual people. Every believer was given breakthrough faith the moment he or she became a Christian. Man does not possess the ability to muster up this faith; God Himself sovereignly and graciously gives it, as it is His faith. The faith that empowers us to believe an impossible Gospel and become a new creation is the same faith that equips us for a sustained lifestyle of supernatural breakthrough.

DECLARE

~~

The words that I speak to you are spirit,
and they are life.—JOHN 6:63

15

DECLARATION STIRS UP FAITH

~~

*And again He entered Capernaum after some days, and
it was heard that He was in the house.* —MARK 2:1

There are three powerful principles of breakthrough faith revealed in
Mark 2:1, and I want to cover them over the next three sections—
declaration, testimony, and Presence. They are all unique keys but
powerfully interrelated. The first one we will focus on is the importance
and power of decree. The words we say can either stir up or stagnate our
faith. This is why in the following pages we are going to explore the biblical balance on what it means to declare words of faith and, as a result,
see God's supernatural power released in our lives.

One of the first things we notice in the paralytic's account is *how*
breakthrough faith is released—through a *decree* or a word. We see *"it
was heard"* that Jesus was in the house. The Message Bible phrases it this
way: *"After a few days, Jesus returned to Capernaum, and word got around
that He was back home"* (Mark 2:1 MSG).

Pay attention to *what* drew the four men to come out to the house
where Jesus was—word got around. It is not stretching the text to say
that the words people were sharing about Jesus were instrumental in
setting up the paralytic for his miracle. As the four men heard decrees

about the miracles Jesus was performing, faith was stirred up within them. They were compelled to bring their friend to Jesus, largely because of the testimony they heard about Him.

A decree awakens and activates faith. Before we study how this all takes place, it is important for us to briefly navigate through some of the controversy and misunderstanding on the topic of declaration and confession.

THE PROBLEM WITH POSITIVE CONFESSION

In the last thirty to forty years of contemporary church history, few things have been as harmful and perverse as the so-called prosperity gospel. This is a major doctrinal ditch we must stay away from. The key is remembering that every road has two sides with two separate ditches— and that both ditches are equally bad. Likewise, it is just as dangerous to equate poverty with spiritual maturity or even sainthood. Prosperity is not the telltale sign of God's blessing, nor is poverty.

Just because people have used "positive confession" language to "name and claim" everything from a new house to a new Bentley to a new spouse does not mean that the power of confession or declaration is of the devil (although the devil would like us to believe it is). To activate the true scriptural power of declaration, we need to see what it is *not*, get a clear picture of what it *is*, and then learn how to apply it in our daily lives. The following chapters are dedicated to help us navigate through this process and start making powerful, biblical declarations of faith.

A decree awakens and activates faith.

I attended a church that was really big into the power of positive confession. For several years I experienced the theological ditch of prosperity gospel, name it and claim it mumbo jumbo, where many people treated God like He was a cosmic butler or a divine vending machine. God was presented as a "get rich quick" principle that we plug our prayers and confessions into in order to get "whatever we need or desire" from Him.

One night when we were leaving a prayer meeting, a group from the church drove past us. Windows open, they were confessing, in faith, that their "new cars were coming." I specifically recall hearing a Cadillac being confessed, and some other fancy brand that I can't remember now. God is not against His children having nice things; however, I am of the opinion that we should not waste our declarations on "calling forth" material stuff; but rather we should invest most of our "confession energy" into agreeing with and declaring the words of Jesus.

Again, I do not believe it is wrong to ask God for big things. Nice things. Needs *and* wants. He is a good Father who longs to bless us in unusual ways. However, when we assume that our declarations order God around and that He is obligated to do whatever we tell Him to, this reveals a life ensnared by serious error and a heart given to lust, not love.

> **Theological controversy should always lead us into a deeper study of Scripture to discover the balance rather than reject an entire truth.**

Remember, when we love Jesus we will imitate Him. When our ears are pressed close to His voice by remaining in His Word and listening to the Holy Spirit, we cannot help but start saying what the Father is saying *through the Son*. By default, we start speaking forth powerful words and declarations that release healing, breakthrough, deliverance, signs, wonders, and miracles. The end result is that our hearts burn to see Jesus receive the glory we know He deserves. We love His glory. We love His supremacy. He alone is our passion. When we treat the name of Jesus as a secret password that obligates God to give us *whatever* we ask Him, love is not our great aim. Instead, we are trying to use God to satisfy our carnal lusts.

After leaving the really off-the-wall positive-confession posse, my wife and I became church vagabonds for an extended season. Through this wandering in the church wilderness, we discovered that *both* ditches were alive and well. After leaving the dysfunctional positive-confession church, we attended another local fellowship where, while trying to appropriately emotionally digest what had just happened in our previous church, we were warned to be careful with what we said, otherwise we might "curse our lives." Again, this represents the imbalance of positive confession.

This perspective believes that if we say a single negative thing, such as, "I don't feel well today," we are literally painting a bull's-eye on our lives for the devil to wreak all sorts of havoc. Let's get this straight: Being negative does not position us to experience a victorious life. But on the flip side, dealing with reality and saying how we feel does not cause God to withdraw His protection and give satan license for a free-for-all in our lives. After visiting a few more churches that tended to be in alignment with the whole positive-confession perspective, we ended up breaking completely from that sphere of Christianity and started attending more traditional churches. It was here that we saw the opposite at work. One camp believed God for everything and another believed Him for nothing.

THE PROBLEM WITH NEGATIVE CONFESSION

The negative confession safeguard is just as dangerous as the positive-confession imbalance. It is common for those who come out of a hyperpositive-confession climate to go completely opposite (I sure did), and instead of believing God for *everything*, they start expecting *nothing*. Here is the bad news: claiming nothing is just as dangerous as claiming everything, for both perspectives completely miss the model of Jesus Christ. He was not silent, nor was He selfish—He simply said what the Father was saying and, in return, saw what the Father was seeing. This is the model we need to follow if we want to stir up breakthrough faith through our declarations.

Negative words simply reveal a mind that needs to be renewed when it comes to the very truths we have discussed so far. Scripture plainly tells us, *"Death and life are in the power of the tongue"* (Prov. 18:21). Jesus made it clear that *"out of the abundance of the heart the mouth speaks"* (Matt. 12:34). Our words are symptomatic of what dwells in our hearts.

In some of the more traditional churches we attended, there was little hope for victory in this lifetime. God was often able but not willing. His ways were mysterious. The devil was not acknowledged as humanity's foe or opponent, and everything bad that happened in life was the result of God's sovereign will and orchestration. There was no fight in the people because there was no fight in their theology. God did *everything*—both good and bad. We noticed a tremendous amount of sickness, torment, and defeat present among those who attended these churches. Too many people were embracing things as legal that the Word of God had declared illegal.

I was living in a wrestling match during this time. I was so burned out by the imbalanced positive-confession stuff, but at the same time, I could not justify sitting back and letting the devil just do whatever he wanted to in my life—and then have the audacity to call it God's will. While I am forever indebted to the season we spent visiting different denominational churches, I became aware of the dire need for a biblical balance. The revelation I received of the cross, the dynamics of salvation, and a hunger for sound theology was truly priceless. However, it was during this same season that I started to ponder, "Could there indeed be a reality where we decide to believe *everything* that is clearly stated in Scripture—from the cross to confession?"

> **Claiming nothing is just as dangerous as claiming everything, for both perspectives completely miss the model of Jesus Christ. He was not silent, nor was He selfish—He simply said what the Father was saying and, in return, saw what the Father was seeing.**

BREAK YOUR AGREEMENT WITH THE DEVIL

One of the keys to walking in breakthrough faith is breaking your agreement with the devil. How can you begin doing this immediately? *Easy. Change your confession.*

I appreciate you hanging in there with me through this controversial chapter. I understand that the subject of positive and negative confession has been taken to wild extremes with some people. Please know that extreme teaching on a particular subject does not make the subject invalid, heretical, or worth rejecting. Oftentimes, some of the most controversial teachings demand our most focused attention. This is one of them.

As we wrap up, I want to present a very sobering reminder. *Negative confession also carries consequences.* Yes, we can actually curse our lives through the words we speak. This does *not* happen by saying something like, "I feel bad today—my stomach is upset." This is *not* saying, "I just don't know how I am going to get through this situation."

Here is an example of a negative confession that could operate as a curse: "My grandfather died young, my father died young, so *I* am going to die young." It is pronouncing a reality over our lives. Maybe it's something like, "My mom had this disease, so I am going to get it too." This is not magic; it's agreement. The devil wants you to make these pronouncements over your life. The question is: Who are you agreeing with by speaking these things? I hope you can tell the difference between saying that you've got a case of the Mondays and announcing that your life is going to be cut short. Negative confessions are attractive to the enemy. More than just speaking arbitrary words, you speak because you actually believe a certain reality. The more you talk about it, the more you reinforce the belief system. This is exactly why the devil would love for you to speak negatively over your life.

Once again, I am not calling for people to deny their circumstances or situations. Denial is *not* faith. Pretending away your problems does not solve them. In fact, pretending you have no problems gives God *nothing* to work with. We must come before the Lord boldly and honestly, presenting our impossibilities before Him. Think about this. Faith does not deny your circumstances; it simply denies your circumstances the place of superior authority and influence over your life. Believe this and speak it.

Your circumstance, situation or impossibility is not definitive. It is not final. It does not and cannot have the last word. It is real, for sure. It is present in your life. It is the wall you are coming against. It is the crowded house that is between you and your breakthrough, just like it was for the four men and their paralyzed friend. I want to repeat it over and over again—faith does not deny your present circumstances. However, faith refuses to consent to the impossible.

This is where negative confession factors into the equation. Negative confession is not expressing how you feel on a particular day; it is you giving up on the possibility of hope and yielding to your circumstance. I encourage you to press through. Break through. You may be thinking, *What about the people who died? What about the people who never saw their breakthroughs? What about the people who hoped and hoped and prayed and believed and never got what they asked for?* These are legitimate questions. Remember, though—circumstances and experiences are not the foundation for your faith and they are not the basis for your confession. Regardless of what is going on around you and in the lives of other people, follow the Psalmist's instructions,

> *I lift up my eyes to the hills.*
> *From where does my help come?*
> *My help comes from the LORD,*
> *who made heaven and earth.*
> (Psalm 121:1-2, ESV)

Lift your eyes. Elevate your perspective. Don't get caught up on what is going on to the left and the right. You are not denying the problem; you are denying the problem's ability to have final say in your life. The Word of God has the final say, and this exactly what you should be declaring and decreeing out of your mouth. It doesn't matter what anyone says. What does God say? Your hope is grounded in the possibilities that the Word of God reveals are available. Your confidence is in the unchanging character and nature of Jesus Christ (see Heb. 13:8).

Think about the 12 spies who scouted out the land of Canaan in Numbers 13. God told them that the land was theirs. The Promise Land was their inheritance! It was not called the Labor Land; it was the Promise Land because God had given it to them through promise. They were being invited to spy it out and claim it. They were not going to have to wrestle it away in some bloodbath with the enemy. Any war they engaged with the inhabitants of the land would be a fixed fight. Why? God had decreed that this land belonged to them and He would not allow anything to prevent them from stepping into this inheritance. Consider how God instructed Moses, *"Send men to spy out the land of Canaan, which I am giving to the children of Israel"* (Num. 13:1). The promise was theirs. The problem? 10 spies made a negative confession because they had an incorrect *perception* of God. They viewed the inhabitants of the land— the opposition and the circumstances against them—as greater than the promise of God, and by default, greater than God Himself. They agreed with the perceived strength of the enemy rather than confidently declaring the limitless and supernatural power of Almighty God. When they made verbal confession of their unbelief, the Bible describes this as *"an evil report of the land"* (Num. 13:32, KJV).

How many people today are confessing an evil report concerning God's promises? No opposition is greater than the God you serve. This is what we have studied so far. Remember, the God Who is infinitely able is also willing. Everything that God *did* throughout Scripture is a reminder that He can *do it again*. Refuse to exalt anything, anyone, or any situation to a position where God becomes inferior to what you are presently going through in life. When we treat God as inferior to anything, we are actually dealing with a false god, since the God of the Bible is infinitely superior to everything we could ever imagine.

I remind you, there is a Biblical balance to this topic of positive and negative confession. At the day's end, I invite you to ask yourself this honest question: *What do you think is more Biblical*—a positive confession that agrees with the Word of God, or a negative confession that agrees with the destructive agenda of satan? Remember, the thief has come to steal, kill and destroy. He desires your agreement. Don't allow him this in-roads. John 10:10 should be the clear standard by which we evaluate the words that come out of our mouths—do they agree with the abundant life that Jesus came to bring, or do they agree with the devil?

The Bible makes it very clear that your words impact your outcomes. In Proverbs 18:21, we see that *"the tongue can bring death or life"* (NLT). Want to know what your world will look like tomorrow? Here is a good place to start—consider your words. Commit to speaking words of life, not death. Agree with the Word of God, not the agenda of the devil. And finally, recognize that any situation or impossibility is inferior to the supernatural power of Almighty God.

THE SECRET TO GOOD SUCCESS

This Book of the Law shall not depart from your mouth, but you shall meditate on it day and night, so that you may be careful to do according to all that is written in it. For then you will make your way prosperous, and then you will have good success. (Joshua 1:8, ESV)

One of the most important keys to your success as a Christian is *declaration* that comes through meditation. You cannot just make a bunch of positive confessions without having a renewed mind. You may confess something that is Biblically true, but if your thinking continues to be un-Biblical, then the overall posture of your thought life will actually undermine what you are confessing.

If you are believing God for physical healing, you may be making positive confessions like: "I am healed because of Jesus' work on the cross" or "Psalm 103 says that God forgives all my sins and heals all my diseases," or "Jesus revealed the will of the Father. He healed everyone, which means the Father's will is to heal me!"

Are these confessions Scripturally true? Yes. Here is my question: Are your confessions birthed in the place of Biblical meditation? Don't let the word "meditate" or meditation concern you. Like all things pure, the enemy has perverted meditation. To some eastern schools of thought and religion, it is an emptying of the mind. This is dangerous because it opens us up to demonic influence. Biblically, to meditate is to think upon, over and over again. When your confession is in alignment with your meditation, the devil will not be able to break your agreement with God's word. Remember, his primary target is your mind. If he can get you to doubt your confession, but you simply continue to speak something forth, almost like a religious formula, it will not benefit you. The Lord intentionally linked meditation and declaration together for Joshua. The same pattern is applicable for you today. Result? *You will have good success!*

Maybe you are different. Perhaps you are thinking, "I *want* my mind to be renewed. I *want* to think like God does. I *want* to have Heaven's perspective on my circumstance…but I'm not there yet." Your confession can actually influence the way you think. It's all about the attitude of your heart. Are you making a positive confession because you think the words by themselves have the ability to deliver the result… without faith attached? Or are you making a positive, Bible-based confession because, even though you are wrestling with doubt, fear, anxiety, or condemnation, it is settled in your heart that God's Word is true and that is what you are going to stand on and announce as final, no matter what happens. When your confession is motivated by that perspective, your words can actually change your thinking to agree with how God thinks. It's almost like your confession is *telling* your mind how to think. Since you earnestly desire a renewed mind, you will hear yourself speaking forth God's Word and your mind will begin to embrace what you are saying.

Ultimately, meditation must produce declaration. A renewed mind should be evidenced in our confession. This is what the Lord describes to Joshua as the Book of the Law not departing from his mouth. The Word of God stays close to Joshua's mouth, as it should for you. When your thought life is under the influence of God's Word, you will say what the Lord is saying. You will declare His decree. Your words will carry Spirit and life because they are the creative, healing, restoring, life-giving Words of God. When your mind is under the influence of the Word of God, your speech will become supernatural.

Your success at the Christian life is not really up to God's sovereignty. Did you know that? He has given you all of the equipment and tools you need to be successful in fulfilling your destiny. It is simply a matter of you stewarding what you have been given. One such thing is your words. The Lord told Joshua that as we meditate upon the Word, confess the Word, and live the Word, *"then you will make your way prosperous, and then you will have good success"* (Josh. 1:8, ESV). Think God's thoughts. Speak God's words. Follow God's instructions. Result? You will experience God's quality of life.

Although this chapter was dedicated to exposing the two extremes of positive confession, we were reminded that the key to stirring up our faith is by *first* possessing a balanced, biblical understanding of this dynamic truth. Because the power of declaration is such a vital way for us to activate breakthrough faith, the first thing we needed to do was clear the air on a controversial topic.

Though there is not ample space in this book to cover this subject in its entirety, the next chapter focuses on one of the most powerful revelations concerning declaration.

POINT OF BREAKTHROUGH

Every theological road has two sides and two ditches—
and both of them are bad. One such road is the power of
positive confession. Instead of throwing out an entire truth,
it is important for us to discover what it is not and what it is
according to Scripture, and learn how to walk in the biblical
balance in order to consistently keep our faith stirred up.

RECOMMENDED READING

The Power of Your Words by Robert Morris

Change Your Words, Change Your Life by Joyce Meyer

Strange Fire, Holy Fire by Michael Klassen

16

AGREEMENT WITH GOD'S WORD RELEASES FAITH

~~

If you abide in Me, and My words abide in you, you will ask what you desire, and it shall be done for you. —JOHN 15:7

In John 15:7 Jesus actually authorizes us to ask for whatever we desire, and then adds on, *"it shall be done for you."* By understanding the principle of agreeing with God's Word, we become equipped to see every impossibility come into alignment and agreement with what God says and what God wills about how a situation *should* work out. Remember, He is the author of faith. He is the author of the very ability that we have to speak forth words of faith, birthed by His Word, that release creative power to supernaturally transform situations. It all starts with what Jesus describes in John 15:7—abiding in His words.

I like how Bill Johnson describes this passage: it is truly like Jesus is giving us a blank check. One has to ask, "What's the catch?" How can Jesus trust us with the offer of a blank check? When we abide in the place of closeness with God, and His words abide, rest, and remain in us, we become fit stewards to fill in the blank check with the very things that are on God's heart.

When our pursuit is God's heart, God's nature, and God's face, our prayers and declarations express this pursuit. Declaration is built on the foundation of friendship with God. It is in the context of relationship with God where His words start to take up residence in our hearts and burn their way into the very fabric of who we are. We want His realities to become manifest on the earth and His Kingdom becomes our great life quest.

Our declarations of agreement with God's Word concerning a situation or circumstance release supernatural power to change whatever we are dealing with. It is not *our* words that have any ability to change things. Think about it. The Holy God has made a way for us mortal human beings to speak forth His immortal words and bring natural circumstances into alignment with supernatural realities. This is truly mind-blowing. Yet, this is what constantly takes place as we recognize that our mouth has become a fit resting place for the transforming power of God's world-creating words.

The major difference between declaring something in faith and going down the positive confession route is that "positive confession often serves as the pretty wrapping paper on a package called denial."[50] God does not invite us to deny the challenges or impossibilities that we face; if He did, then when breakthrough was released, He would not receive the glory due His name. This is the tragedy of imbalanced positive confession theology.

I once heard of a healing evangelist who was trying to pray for a woman with a terminal disease. The woman would not acknowledge the disease, claiming that her pastor told her to not make a negative confession. The evangelist was not impressed with her line of thinking because it is a "glory thief." God gets glory when we invite Him into a situation that requires divine adjustment. When we live in denial, we are pretending that everything is okay and that by maintaining our positive confession we can simply pretend the problem away. Denying reality solves nothing and ultimately gives God *no glory* whatsoever.

When our three-fold pursuit is God's heart, God's nature, and God's face, our prayers and declarations express this pursuit.

WORDS RELEASE SUPERNATURAL CREATIVE POWER

Jesus spoke what He first heard spoken in Heaven. This is a fundamental key to releasing breakthrough faith through our prayers, confessions, and decrees. Jesus' words were constant "amens" of agreement to what Father God was saying. May we follow this model with our words and declarations as well. What an incredible example we have been given in our Savior who stated, *"The words that I speak to you are spirit, and they are life"* (John 6:63).

Declaration is a direct result of our intimacy with God, and, ultimately, it is the offspring of a renewed mind. What is in our hearts and in our minds will come out of our mouths. When this happens, we become positioned to release the very life and power of God through our declarations. This is exactly what happened with Jesus. His words actually became spirit and life as He spoke out of a place of closeness with the Father.

When we start speaking what we hear God saying, much like Jesus did, then our words are no longer merely verbal statements. We go beyond sentences, phrases, and grammar. When our words are in sync and in agreement with what God the Father is presently saying in Heaven, these very words take on the same quality that Jesus' did. They actually become "spirit and life." They announce realities, and go on to actually create the realities they announce. They declare a heavenly decree, and also unleash the very power to bring the decree to pass.

Somehow, the very Spirit of God was released upon the words of Jesus. The same Spirit lives inside of you and me, which means that we have been invited into the same supernatural experience that Jesus lived in. His words created and destroyed. They created hope, life, healing, deliverance, and freedom while destroying torment, sickness, bondage, fear, and condemnation. Our words, in and of themselves, explain, communicate, and encourage. However, when the words of Heaven flow out of our mouths, Heaven starts transforming the earth.

This is not some pie-in-the-sky, fantasy approach to life. We need to work hard. We need to be good stewards of what we have been given.

We need to make wise choices and wise decisions, and not simply think, "Well, if I confess to be debt-free, I will be!" Our positive confession will not pay the light bill or turn our marriage around in an hour. We need to take practical, biblical steps towards walking in these solutions, all the while verbally agreeing with the very heartbeat of God.

Too many faith preachers have led countless Christians into deception, promising that giving a certain amount of money or confessing a certain Bible promise so many times a day is the surefire solution to all earthly woes. No. Declaration does release supernatural solutions, but these solutions are born in the secret place of intimacy with the Father.

It is an intimate relationship with God that produces imitation. The more we live in God's Presence, the more our hearts burn for His nearness. Our love for Him increases because our love for Him is always responsive—we love Him because He first loved us (see 1 John 4:19). We draw near to Him because He made the first move toward us while we were still sinners (see Rom. 5:8). We change in response to who He is and how we encounter Him. We are awestruck by His beauty. We are amazed by His power. We are humbled by His holiness. We are undone by His grace and mercy.

The knowledge of God compels us to know this Glorious One who delivered us out of darkness and, through the blood of Jesus, translated us into a whole new Kingdom (see Col. 1:13). We burn to know Him. We yearn to spend time with Him. And as the apostle Paul wrote, time in God's Presence, simply beholding the One we love, transforms us into His image and likeness from one degree of glory to the next (see 2 Cor. 3:18). The more we get to know Him, the more accurately we will be able to represent Him.

> **When the words of Heaven flow out of our mouths, Heaven starts transforming the earth.**

One of the ways we follow Jesus' example is through our words. In fact, our words are one of the most blatant ways that reveal our level of agreement with God's Word. In Hebrews 13:5-6 we read, *"For He*

Himself has said, 'I will never leave you nor forsake you.' So we may boldly say: 'The Lord is my helper; I will not fear. What can man do to me?'"

The author of Hebrews gives us a clear model on how to imitate God through our words. We simply say what God says: *"For He Himself has said...so we may boldly say...."* We declare what has *already been* said by God. I appreciate that the author added in the word "boldly." If God, the One who is faithful, true, unchanging, and perfect, says something, then we can declare it with boldness and confidence. We can expect such words to produce fruit because they are not our words; they are God's! Even Jesus, the very Son of God, unveiled this lifestyle of speaking *only* what God first said. Jesus' words modeled complete agreement with God, as He made it clear that He did not speak on His own authority (see John 12:49; 14:10). He said at one point, *"So whatever I speak, I am saying [exactly] what My Father has told Me to say and in accordance with His instructions"* (John 12:50 AMP). Jesus did not say whatever He wanted to whenever He felt like it, expecting that the Father would bring these words to pass just because He "confessed them in faith." Jesus Christ faithfully spoke the words of the One He loved and enjoyed precious fellowship with—the Father.

The incredible truth is that you and I have also been summoned into this union of power and love. We enjoy fellowship with the Father because His love has called us into His Presence. It is out of this place of relationship that we speak what our Beloved has first said. This experience was not exclusively reserved for Jesus Christ alone, but is also available to all who would say "yes" to the Father's royal invitation. If the apostle Paul could experience this, so can you and I!

Paul wrote, *"And my speech and my preaching were not with persuasive words of human wisdom, but in demonstration of the Spirit and of power, that your faith should not be in the wisdom of men but in the power of God"* (1 Cor. 2:4-5). When Paul preached, natural human words did not just come out of his mouth. People were not touched by the eloquence of his speech or articulation of his oratory. When this man opened his mortal mouth, it became a conduit for the immortal Word of God.

His lips become a gateway for the power of Heaven. Paul preached God's message—the Gospel. When we declare what God is saying, our words release His supernatural power. In fact, the words *become* power. Remember what Jesus said in John 6:63—*"The words that I speak to you are spirit, and they are life"*? Jesus' words in our mouths carried by our speech release *God's* supernatural creative power!

THREE KEYS TO RELEASING GOD'S POWER THROUGH DECLARATION

Stepping into Our Identity

> Then God said, "Let Us make man in Our image, according to Our likeness; let them have dominion..." (Genesis 1:26).

The first key to releasing God's power through declaration is to understand that when we declare things by faith, *we are actually stepping into our identity as ones fashioned in the image and likeness of Creator God.* In addition, declarations that are in agreement with the image and likeness of God release His will into circumstances that are out of order. Divine order is alignment with God's will and Heaven's culture. When we face situations in our lives that are out of order with God's perfect will, we need to step into this identity and begin declaring God's order and God's solutions. This is our starting place. Remember, we do not deny the problems we are experiencing; we are simply confronting them with our declarations of faith that are in agreement with God's Word.

Paul reminds us that our God is the One who *"who gives life to the dead and calls those things which do not exist as though they did"* (Rom. 4:17). How do we respond to this dimension of God's character and nature, as a person who speaks Heaven's realities into dead places and produces order and creation? We start by combining this truth with another one Paul reveals: *"Therefore be imitators of God as dear children"* (Eph. 5:1).

We are invited to imitate the One who calls things that do not exist as though they do. The things we are "calling into existence" are not

Rolex watches and sports cars. We know what we are licensed to "decree into existence" through the written Word of God combined with the revealed nature and character of God in Jesus Christ. People "proof text" the Bible all of the time, taking a verse here or a verse there, and somehow twisting it into a passage that makes their selfish positive confessions legal. No. This cannot be. This process is much more than just knowing Bible verses and applying them to specific problems. It is actually having our hearts, minds, and words oriented to the heart, mind, and words of Father God.

> ## Jesus' words in our mouth carried by our speech release *God's* supernatural creative power!

Stirs Up Faith

The second key to releasing God's power through declaration is recognizing that *declaration stirs up the breakthrough faith within us.* We are to remember that faith is already on the inside of us. The supernatural ability to move mountains is not something special we need to climb the spiritual ladder for. Our confession does *not* give us more faith, as some people teach. It is impossible for us to receive "more faith" because we have already received the very faith of God!

We are to stir up and release what is already within us! When we start making declarations and confessions that are in agreement with the very nature and Word of God, something supernatural takes place inside of us. The potential of our faith is awakened and unlocked.

Think of what happened when God initiated creation. God Himself spoke, in faith, to bring the seen out of the unseen—reality out of nothingness. A spoken decree preceded a tangible reality. In Genesis 1:3 we read, *"Then God said, 'Let there be light'; and there was light."* First, God *said;* then light came. God had faith that this thing called creation was going to work out, but there was obviously some supernatural collision that took place when words proceeded out of His mouth. They gave expression to the faith that was in His heart; God had faith in Himself and in His ability, and rightly so! We are called to model this very kind of faith in Him. This is the faith we have inherited: world-creating faith!

Now picture this: the very faith that brought creation into being actually resides on the inside of us. For us to accept the redemptive work of Jesus Christ and become a Christian, we need to believe that our profession of faith in Christ has the power and ability to produce a specific result—*re-creating us*. We essentially believe that by making Jesus our Lord and Savior, we are being re-created in His image. Scripture says that when we are born again, we become a new creation in Christ (see 2 Cor. 5:17). In order for us to get saved to begin with, we actually require the very faith of God that created the world, for we are placing our trust in a unique, supernatural creative process of its own. It is the re-creative process of redemption. And the good news is that if we are saved, if we are a believer in the Lord Jesus Christ, *then we have this faith already inside of us*!

Kinetic Supernatural Power

The third key to releasing God's power through declaration is that when *we activate this God-sized faith through our declaration, potential faith changes into kinetic supernatural power*. I know a lot of people who have declared and confessed Scripture until they were blue in the face—and ultimately, "blue in the faith." The main problem was not necessarily with *what* they were confessing; unfortunately, they were speaking things out of their mouths that they did not ultimately believe in their hearts.

There are people who have verbally "confessed" Christ who are still not true believers. Words matter little unless there is the vital substance of belief reinforcing those words. I could confess "I love mayonnaise" all day long, every day, for the rest of my life. But I guarantee you, this declaration would not compel me to love, like, or even tolerate the stuff because I would not believe what I am saying.

Everything in the Kingdom of God starts in the heart. Remember, our hearts believe realities about God and His Kingdom as we pursue intimacy with Him. When our hearts stand in agreement with the realities of His Kingdom, and when our mouths give voice to these truths through declaration, something powerful happens in the spirit realm. As we studied earlier, these Heaven-birthed words actually *become* life and supernatural power.

Let me illustrate this point. In science there is potential and kinetic energy. Potential energy is exactly what the name implies—it contains the potential for motion and action. I love how one website described potential energy, as "energy ready to go."[51] Faith is supernatural power that is ready to go. However, it requires action. Scripture tells us that faith without works is dead and dormant (see James 2:17-18). In fact, faith without corresponding expression is really a sham. It is poor stewardship of the supernatural gift of God living within us. It lives in this perpetual state of being *ready to go,* but sadly, it is never released and transformed into kinetic faith—supernatural power.

The very faith that brought creation into being actually resides on the inside of us.

One such action that puts faith to work is declaration. Real-life examples of potential energy include a lawn mower filled with gasoline, a car on top of a hill, and students waiting to come home from school. All of these examples are stationary, *but* they are all ready for some catalyst to set them into action. Potential energy becomes *kinetic* when it is set into motion. A lawnmower requires a spark before it roars to life. In the same way, our faith is activated by the spark of the Father's words proceeding out of our mouths. God spoke, and light was.

In the next section I want us to study a key "spark" to igniting breakthrough faith. What was the catalyst that activated breakthrough faith for the four men with their paralyzed friend in Mark 2? *"Something was heard."* We have just finished exploring the vital process of what happens when this "something" is spoken aloud and declared. But what exactly is the "something" that we need to be speaking?

There is an ancient secret that carries over from the Old Testament into the New. If practiced this will take the church into a whole new dimension of supernatural power and authority. The body of Christ is like that lawnmower filled to the brim with spiritual gasoline. What's missing? That vital, catalytic spark of ignition. What pushes faith out of the potential into the kinetic? What causes four guys to have such extraordinary, out-of-the-box faith that they break through a roof and lower their friend down just to get to Jesus? Testimony.

POINT OF BREAKTHROUGH

The secret to making Bible-based, power-producing declarations is enjoying intimate fellowship with Jesus. By being close to Him, we clearly hear His words and our passion is to imitate Him by saying what He is saying. When we speak the words of Jesus, we are speaking the words of God and His words alone release supernatural power.

~~~

RECOMMENDED READING

Dreaming with God by Bill Johnson

God's Creative Power by Charles Capps

Testify

~~

Blessed are those who keep His
testimonies. —Psalm 119:2

17

STUDYING TESTIMONY AWAKENS FAITH

~~

And again He entered Capernaum after some days, and
it was heard that He was in the house. —MARK 2:1

Breakthrough faith incited the paralytic's four friends to take action, but it was hearing the testimonies and stories of Jesus' works that awakened their faith to begin with. Oftentimes, it takes a simple declaration of testimony to transition our faith from being potential to going kinetic, from being "in waiting mode" to releasing measurable miraculous breakthroughs. We are going to explore this topic in the next few chapters, as it is the testimony that awakens the supernatural, prophetic power of faith in our hearts.

We see in Mark 2:1 that testimony about Jesus was spreading throughout the city. Surely, people often spoke of His miraculous power. I am certain that stories were exchanged of how He healed the sick, set people free from demonic torment, and turned impossible situations around. It goes without saying that the four guys (with their paralyzed friend) were exposed to a culture that is so desperately needed in the church today—a culture of storytelling and testimony.

We know that people were sharing these miraculous stories because we go on to see the by-product of everyone talking about the arrival of

Jesus: *"Immediately many gathered together"* (Mark 2:2). Testimonies of the miraculous are divine invitations for people to experience the Miracle Maker for themselves. Something was *heard* that caused these four friends to lower their paralyzed friend through a roof in order to get to Jesus. Thus begs the question, What was heard that compelled the four men to behave so radically? Testimony.

> **Oftentimes, it takes a simple declaration of testimony to transition our faith from being potential to going kinetic.**

TESTIMONY BIRTHS RELENTLESS HOPE ACROSS NATIONS

As we begin to study testimony, let us begin with a big vision. Historically, when a region, city, or area experienced a powerful in-breaking of the Holy Spirit, which was often accompanied with mass conversions, signs, wonders, and supernatural phenomena, testimony of that activity would start to spread like wildfire. Whether we are talking about the day in which Jesus lived or twenty-first-century society, the power of testimony produces global shifts in the culture of faith. These shifts begin when everyday people like you and me hear what God is doing (or has done), and we start pressing in to experience the same realities in our spheres of influence.

Time after time, when believers in different geographies *heard* about what God was doing in certain hotbeds of spiritual activity, the testimony did something to all who read it, heard it, and received it. It was like the stories of God's mighty exploits deposited relentless hope inside of these people. Though separated by continents, oceans, and sometimes eras in history, one common denominator connects all those who heard testimony of what God was doing: they all experienced hope that awakened breakthrough faith to believe God for history-making revival.

Remember, hope arises within us as we are exposed to possibilities that were previously off the radar. Hope gives us a new supernatural set of options. Before they are introduced to hope, believers are often just plugging away, doing what they know to do with the resources think they have. Then suddenly they hear of a fresh wind of the Spirit blowing in a different part of the world. Or they read a book about a historic revivalist or move of God that changed the landscape of a society. These testimonies become our fuel for breakthrough faith. Personally, I cannot escape the subject.

My interest in the theme of testimony began back in 2010, when I took a class dedicated to surveying the global activity and movement of the Holy Spirit throughout history. I was absolutely awestruck at how reports of the miracles and works of God spread throughout the earth. This was back before the Internet, before live-streaming technology, before cable television, and yes, even before radio. This was back when testimony was transmitted through print media, such as newspapers, magazines, and even letters. The method is not all that important; it is the incredible results that continually stir my heart.

I cannot help but think of the nation-shaking Welsh Revival of 1904 and its global impact. Revival historian Wesley Duewel noted that "the wind of the Holy Spirit carried the revival fire from nation to nation as *the wonderful news of the revival in Wales* reached prayer groups in many parts of the world."[52] What carried this revival fire? It was the power of testimony.

One of the greatest moves of God in recent history, the Azusa Street Revival, spread to the nations through the transmission of testimony as well. William Seymour, one of the key leaders at Azusa Street, had a periodical entitled *Apostolic Faith*, "which reached an international circulation of 50,000 at its peak in 1908…hundreds of visitors from all over the continent and internationally came to see what was happening and to be baptized in the Spirit."[53]

Hope gives us a new supernatural set of options.

Such reports release new possibilities of God breaking into entire communities, converting people in masses, performing creative miracles, growing out missing body parts, manifesting His Presence visibly, and filling people with a fresh baptism of the Holy Spirit. Again, those who heard testimony were exposed to new options. They had hope awakened deep within their hearts. But that was not enough for them. They allowed that hope to develop into breakthrough faith.

The people who heard about these mighty acts of God become discontent living to pursue the *possible*. They celebrated what God had done and was doing—and then pressed in to experience it for themselves. Duewel further explained that "as news of God's mighty work in Wales reached them, Christians and Christian leaders in other places renewed and multiplied their efforts to seek the Lord *until He answered*. Holy hunger and thirst were deepened. Holy zeal was fanned into flame, and encouragement and expectancy filled many hearts."[54]

Testimony exposes us to new realities and births within us a fiery spiritual tenacity. This is what creates a people who seek God until they actually find Him. This is what shapes revivalists. We catch a vision of what God has done and we become discontent settling for anything beneath *everything* that He wants to do in our lives, communities, cities, and nations.

Three Testimony Truths that Will Awaken Breakthrough Faith

> *Trust in the Lord, and do good; dwell in the land, and feed on His faithfulness* (Psalm 37:3).

While there are no levels of faith, there are practical ways to steward the faith we have already received. Here are three practical keys so that we can allow testimony to powerfully shape our faith and position us for a lifestyle of breakthrough.

Testimony Is Prophecy

First, we must understand that *testimony is a prophecy of what God will do again*. We read in Revelation 19:10 that *"the testimony of Jesus is the spirit of prophecy."* When we declare testimony of what Jesus is doing or has done—from saving souls to healing bodies to transforming entire communities—we are actually prophesying what He will do again. Just as a prophecy can foretell a future event, testimony of what God has done in the past actually foretells what He can and will do again. How do we know that He will do what He has already done? It is His very nature to do so. Hebrews 13:8 reminds us, *"Jesus Christ is the same yesterday, today, and forever."*

Why do evangelistic outreaches often have people featured on stage, sharing their salvation testimony, talking about how they first came to know Jesus? The ministries or churches putting on the event are hoping that a particular person's testimony will resonate with unbelievers in attendance, and let them know, "If God did this for me, then He can do it for *you*. If He saved me, He can and will save you."

The Bible tells us that *"God is no respecter of persons"* (Acts 10:34 KJV). What He did for one person, He can and will to do for the next. He is simply revealing who He is, and that does not change. There is something about a person sharing testimony of what God has done in his or her life that releases a fresh revelation of God's nearness, power, and reality. It brings Scripture into 3-D.

Our testimonies are not a replacement for Scripture; they actually illustrate it. They prove that the Word of God works. When we experience realities that are written about in the Scriptures, we *must* share them, for our experiences demonstrate the reliability and relevance of God's Word. It is not just a book to be engaged with mentally, but it is a legal document that shows us everything that is available for us to experience in God's Kingdom.

Testimony Witnesses Who God Is

The second truth about testimony that will awaken faith within us is that *testimony is a witness of who God is*. Bill Johnson observes, "We are never the main characters in a testimony."[55] In Hebrew, the word *testimony* comes from the term 'edah, which describes a testimony or witness. When God does something and it becomes a story to tell, the story actually gives expression and witness to who God is and what He is like. We praise Him for His acts but it never ends with what He did. His acts are to be pondered and considered, for they unveil who He is.

This is so important. Many well-meaning people urge us, "Don't seek God's hand; seek His face." While there is some truth here, the problem with repeating this statement so often is that it dampens a believer's hunger for the demonstration of God's supernatural acts. The key is perspective. If we are just looking for a cool show, then yes, we are not mature enough to pursue God's acts, for it does not end with Him. Instead, it ends with the miracle, with something getting fixed, healed, or restored. It ends with man's wholeness, not God's glory. God desires to release a torrent of supernatural activity through His church into the earth, unlike anything we've seen before. We are not waiting on Heaven; Heaven is waiting on the church and looking for a people with hearts that burn for Him alone.

Jesus is the ultimate example of this glorious witness to God's nature. Everything He did revealed who the Father was. Paul notes that Jesus *"is the image of the invisible God"* (Col. 1:15). And in Hebrews 1:3 we see that *"the Son radiates God's own glory and expresses the very character of God"* (NLT). Jesus explained it most clearly when He said, *"I tell you the truth, the Son can do nothing by Himself; He can do only what He sees His Father doing, because whatever the Father does the Son also does. For the Father loves the Son and shows Him all He does"* (John 5:19-20 NIV).

Jesus was the living embodiment of testimony. Everything He did—healing the sick, raising the dead, delivering people from demonic torment, loving the unlovely, touching the untouchable, silencing accusations, disarming condemnation—gave physical, visible expression to who God the Father was. This is why Jesus had to smile, and perhaps shake his head a little when Philip said to Him, *"Lord, show us the Father, and it is sufficient for us"* (John 14:8). Patiently and lovingly Jesus responded, *"You've been with me all this time, Philip, and you still don't understand? To see Me is to see the Father"* (John 14:9 MSG).

Testimony Keeps Future Generations Connected to God's Reality

The third truth about testimony that will help awaken faith within us is that *testimony keeps future generations connected to the reality of God.*

This is why stories of God's supernatural interventions, signs, wonders, miracles, and breakthroughs are so important for us to continually rehearse. They are not secondary elements in the Christian experience. Testimonies are nourishment for future generations to feed on God's faithfulness. They become living springs for our children to draw from, not merely to memorialize something that happened back in the day, but as a prophetic promise assuring future generations that what happened then can and will *happen again.*

The same testimony that stirred four men to bust through a ceiling is what we are called to declare to this generation—and the generations to come. In Psalm 78:5-7 we read:

> *For He established a testimony in Jacob, and appointed a law in Israel, which He commanded our fathers, that they should make them known to their children; that the generation to come might know them, the children who would be born, that they may arise and declare them to their children, that they may set their hope in God, and not forget the works of God.*

Testimonies are nourishment for future generations to feed on God's faithfulness.

Again, Psalm 145:4 reminds us of our generational responsibility: *"One generation shall praise Your works to another, and shall declare Your mighty acts."* We must connect future generations with testimony of what God is doing and has done in the past. This is an area where the church has been somewhat weak in its recent years. We assume that we are "feeding" our young people through a steady diet of principle-based sermons, community activities, fellowship, fun and games, modern worship, and the like. None of these are bad in and of themselves—they are just useless when they are divorced from a culture of testimony. We need to start telling a generation about the ear-tingling works of almighty God once again. Remember, He is the One who declared, *"Behold, I will do something in Israel at which both ears of everyone who hears it will tingle"* (1 Sam. 3:11).

We need to talk about the stories of miracles, signs, and wonders, where eyeballs appeared back in their sockets, limbs grew out where they were absent, and missing organs were supernaturally re-created. We need to share about the mighty revivals, where the Presence and power of God so powerfully fell upon a community that culture shifted. Darkness was subdued. Sinful activities diminished.

We need to testify of the men and women who recognized they walked under an open Heaven. They were not extraordinary. They were not celebrities. In fact, they were no different than you and me. Charles Spurgeon commented, "Whenever God has done a mighty work it has been by some very insignificant instrument."[56] The reformers and revivalists of old were simply people who lived with conviction. They recognized that Heaven was open over their lives and lived like it was true. They recognized that the breakthrough faith of God was inside of them to work the impossible—and they pressed in to actually experience it.

THE ALTERNATIVE TO FEEDING ON TESTIMONY

The generation that walks in a normal lifestyle of breakthrough faith is the generation that feeds on God's testimonies as vital nourishment for sustaining spiritual life. Unfortunately, there is an opposite perspective that renders us powerless. When we are not constantly sharing testimony of what God is doing, He starts to seem distant. Is He really distant? Of course He isn't.

The interesting thing is that testimony actually directs our view of God. As we focus on testimonies of His power and His mighty acts, we are reminded of His nearness and reality. When we are disconnected from testimony, however, we are disconnected from Him. God becomes a mere concept. He is surely out there—somewhere—but not close at hand. Perhaps we do not question His reality, but we may start responding to Him as though He is disinterested and uninvolved in our lives.

At all costs, we must avoid a culture where testimony is absent. If we do not continue to declare the works of the Lord, we run the risk of building spiritual culture like the one described in the book of Judges.

> *The people worshiped God throughout the lifetime of Joshua and the time of the leaders who survived him, leaders who had been in on all of God's great work that He had done for Israel. Then Joshua son of Nun, the servant of God, died. He was 110 years old. They buried him in his allotted inheritance at Timnath Heres in the hills of Ephraim north of Mount Gaash.*

> *Eventually that entire generation died and was buried. Then another generation grew up that didn't know anything of God or the work He had done for Israel. The people of Israel did evil in God's sight* (Judges 2:7-11 MSG).

A generation becomes prone to do evil in God's sight when they are disconnected from a continuous feast on His acts, wonders, and supernatural exploits. In the chapters ahead we will study the power of sharing testimony, why developing a culture of testimony is so important in our lives and churches, and, finally, we will review some practical ways we can start building this type of faith-stirring environment.

POINT OF BREAKTHROUGH

By studying testimony of Jesus' acts, wonders, and miracles, we awaken the breakthrough faith that God placed within us. Stories of what God has done in the past, or what He is doing in other places, show us what is possible in our lives and in our world today. By constantly reviewing these stories, our faith is awakened to believe that the same God who moved will move again.

RECOMMENDED READING

There is More by Randy Clark

Revival Fire by Wesley Duewel

True Stories of the Miracles of Azusa Street and Beyond
by Tommy Welchel and Michelle Griffith

18

SHARING TESTIMONY IGNITES FAITH

~~~

Storyteller: a person who invites others to enter the experience of a story. —MARK MILLER[57]

Long before I was involved in ministry, I was a storyteller. I received my bachelor's degree in script and screenwriting. I was a movie junkie for many, many years. However, I could not decide what route I wanted to pursue in the industry. Part of me wanted to take a stab at film journalism. I wanted to be a movie critic like Siskel and Ebert (from back in the day). The other part of me wanted to *tell* stories through writing screenplays. I tried my hand at both, assuming that I was well on my way to a career in some form of entertainment media. But then the Presence and power of God rocked me. That said, my heart still burns to see revival in Hollywood and an age of creative renaissance break forth in the church.

Telling story is a powerful tool, both for good and for evil. Story stirs us up. It exposes us to possibilities that were previously off our radars. It awakens hope and, yes, even releases breakthrough faith. This is the essence of testimony.

WE ARE SUPERNATURAL STORYTELLERS

The greatest, most powerful expression of storytelling that *each* of us possess is the power of *our* testimony. Testimony takes place as God writes His story in and through our lives.

For all Christians, testimony begins with something that we all have in common—our salvation experience. However, testimony does not end here. In many contexts, we have limited the concept of "testimony" to one's salvation story. This should not be the case. If you have a story of God doing the miraculous and supernatural in your life, or of God using you to release His power to someone else, you have become a steward of that testimony. Remember what Jesus said: *"Freely you have received, freely give"* (Matt. 10:8). Jesus is saying that what you received from Him becomes yours to give away to others. One of the primary ways you "freely give" is by telling your story and sharing your testimony.

If God has moved supernaturally in your life, then congratulations—you have become a supernatural storyteller. There are so many different ways each of us can tell our stories. I read Mark Miller's book *Experiential Storytelling* and it opened my eyes to the myriad of ways we can communicate the supernatural stories of God. The book reminded me of the great need for the stories of God's awesome deeds to be shared again from the body of Christ. Not just pleasant anecdotes and jokes. We need to have a clear vision of what story is and what will happen when we share the stories of God's miraculous invasions in our lives.

> **Testimony takes place as God writes His story in and through our lives.**

OLD-TIME TESTIFYIN'

Telling our stories ignites the spark of breakthrough faith that resides in every believer within "hearing" range (there are multiple ways one can hear our testimony). Remember, breakthrough faith is already on the inside of every believer. It is not some special faith upgrade we need to receive from a spiritual celebrity. However, it often lays dormant inside of us for far too long—in potential form—until a spark ignites it and makes it kinetic. This is what sharing our story does. It ignites the spark of faith within others to believe for what God has done for us.

I began to recognize the prophetic power of testimony as I studied the mighty moves of God throughout history. How were people able to *feed* on the testimonies of God's Presence and power, thus transforming entire regions? The people who experienced the fire of revival, firsthand, *told* their stories. They wrote about these testimonies in publications, periodicals, and letters. People connected and dialogued with them. It was *heard* that God was moving! It was as simple as that. We cannot contain the supernatural work of the Holy Spirit by keeping it to ourselves—all of us are called to talk about what God is doing in our lives.

Back in the not-so-distant past of church culture, they held what were called "testimony services." These often took place on either a Wednesday or Sunday night and would consist of an entire church service dedicated to people sharing testimonies of what God had done in their lives. Oh, that we would recognize the dire need for such an outlet in the body of Christ today! Christians are absolutely overwhelmed with teaching and information. I am not disregarding the need for teaching; I am just saying that a time needs to come where people actually start *experiencing* what the preacher has been teaching about.

In Mark 2:2 we see that testimony about Jesus' works circulated and the result was that *"many were gathered together, so that there was no more room, not even at the door"* (ESV). Preaching and teaching *must* be reinforced with testimony, as testimony reveals what is possible to the person who applies what is being taught from Scripture. I have to believe that in Jesus' day, people had their own version of "testimony services."

Story after story in the Gospels points to this reality; the results speak for themselves. As stories were shared, the miracles multiplied. People, like the four men with the paralytic friend, caught wind of what Jesus was doing, and those testimonies prophesied over them about what was possible. The stories of Jesus' miracles and mighty works declared, loud and clear, that if He did it for that one guy or girl back then, then He can and will do it for us as well. For many of these stories were sparks that ignited bold quests and radical pursuits for an encounter with Jesus. The key was keeping testimony in front of the people as a matter of significant importance. In Bible times this was their culture. In our day, it is often a struggle.

Many times we live unexposed to the supernatural possibilities of God's power. We live distanced from God healing people miraculously, delivering them from torment, freeing their minds, breaking addictions, restoring families, setting people free from demonic oppression, raising the dead, and the like. When we do not hear testimony of God doing these things *today*, it becomes easy to start believing a bunch of nonsense theology: *God does not do miraculous things anymore, He only moves overseas, and the supernatural is not available to everyday believers.*

Silence concerning God's works actually fosters false doctrine about God's supernatural power. We cannot afford to keep our stories quiet, as that is exactly what the enemy would love for us to do. The truth is that God is moving powerfully across the world, even in our nation! Undoubtedly, He is moving in your life as well. Do not keep His goodness to yourself. As you share what He is doing, your stories become sparks that ignite breakthrough faith for others to believe God for the impossible!

Testimony reveals what is possible to the person who applies what is being taught in Scripture.

TESTIMONY: THE MISSING LINK IN MODERN CHRISTIANITY

Miracles have become a missing link in much of Western church culture today. This is *not* because God made a sovereign withdrawal of His power from the earth, but rather because the church has remained silent when it comes to the testimony of God's supernatural interventions. They are frequent, rest assured. They are both simple and spectacular. Sadly, we have become overly skeptical or just plain silent.

In Mark 2:1-2 we note that the crowd gathered to see and hear Jesus because of what they heard about Him. This says that we need to *gather* and *assemble* around the testimony once again. This was undeniably the church culture in the Book of Acts. They were committed to testifying of what the Holy Spirit was doing in their midst, and, as a result, entire regions and cities were touched by God's power.

To experience a fresh move of the Holy Spirit, we need to return to the foundations of our faith. For too long the central focus of our meetings has been delivering Bible-based principles via sermons. While we cannot neglect the truth that comes from the time-tested precepts of Scripture, we must start building a culture around the present-day works of God. The miracles in our midst. The acts of God in our cities, regions, churches, and nations. Could it be that cities are not being transformed by the supernatural power of God because churches are *not* sharing their stories?

In the present-day church era, people have exchanged powerful testimony for weak principles. People are not usually invited to church to hear about the person who was healed of cancer, or the marriage that was restored, or the demon-possessed individual who was liberated. And yet this was a major draw in the Gospels. People were powerfully transformed and discipled as a result of hearing stories of the miracles that Jesus performed. We must remember that the Bible is more testimony-driven than principle-based. Biblical principles were often birthed out of supernatural encounters people had with God.

There is a significant pattern for us to observe in testimony and how sharing it impacts our relationship with God and the expression of our faith. Bill Johnson writes concerning this, "When we forget about the miracles, we talk about them less. And if our expectations of the miraculous decline, miracles eventually disappear from our lives altogether."[58]

The Bible is more testimony-driven than principle-based. Biblical principles were often birthed out of supernatural encounters people had with God.

Miracles, Revival, and Testimony

God loves *giving us* illustrated sermons. As I studied about testimony in my class, God decided to illustrate the lesson through a real-life situation. During this season, something remarkable was brewing in Mobile, Alabama. On July 23, 2010, the last day of Church of His Presence's "Open the Heavens" conference, God did exactly what they were asking for. Revival broke out, the glory of God invaded that conference hall, and powerful miracles started to become normative in their gatherings. Deaf ears and blind eyes were opening. People were getting saved and rededicating their lives to Jesus Christ. There was joy and reverence, holiness, and power.

And one of the most notable miracles to take place was the supernatural healing of a paralyzed woman named Delia Knox. She had been in a wheelchair since Christmas Day 1987, when she got in a near-fatal car accident resulting from a drunk driver. She received prayer at the revival—not in some flamboyant, "let's pull her up out of the wheelchair" way, but in a very honoring and Jesus-exalting manner. The result was that she was completely healed of her paralyzed condition!

Not long after her healing, she came up on stage and testified to what God has done in her life—before a live audience and to thousands watching around the world through Internet streaming and television.[59] Her testimony released hope and healing to more people than we will ever know this side of Heaven. Most importantly, her story reminds us of why we need to intentionally pursue building a culture of testimony in our churches today. Declaring testimony ignites the spark that releases and sustains the consuming fire of breakthrough faith.

Declaring Testimony Puts the Bible in 3-D

Simply reading the Bible does not awaken faith; it is awakened when we are exposed to the Bible *in the flesh*. When people share testimony of what God has done or what He is doing, it takes what we read about in Scripture and displays it in 3-D. The Bible was never meant to be read like a textbook or history book; it is *alive* and active (see Heb. 4:12).

The more a generation mistakenly believes that Christianity is all about sitting in a room, reading a book, doing a devotional, or listening to a preacher, the more detached they will become from authentic New Testament faith. This is because they are being exposed to a counterfeit version of Christianity. Are the elements I listed above *part* of our Christian experience? Yes, but when these few elements are presented as "the entire Christian package," we are being introduced to a subpar version of what Jesus died for and what He sent the Holy Spirit to give us. By sharing testimony, we let a generation know that there is *more* to Christianity than what some would lead them to believe, and that there is more to the Bible than just sitting around and reading a book.

One way we can experience the life of Scripture is when we hear people share what the Word has actually produced in their lives! The Bible cannot just be the "good book." It cannot just be information we store up in our brains only to regurgitate on a test, in a Bible study, or through preaching a sermon. Our inheritance as believers is a Word that produces *life*. Review yet again what Jesus said about His words—they are spirit and they are life (see John 6:63). And recall the apostle Paul, whose preaching was not delivered with brilliant oration or flowery eloquence, but with *supernatural power* (see 1 Cor. 2:4-5). *This* is the expression of Christianity we have been destined to bring to this world!

In the next and final chapter about testimony, we will get really practical. How do we make sharing testimony a lifestyle rather than an occasional two-minute video break during a Sunday service?

Our inheritance as believers is a Word that produces *life*.

POINT OF BREAKTHROUGH

By sharing our stories of God's supernatural works—no matter how big or small—our testimonies release sparks that ignite breakthrough faith to believe God for the miraculous. We cannot afford to keep silent about what Jesus has done in our lives. In fact, someone else's breakthrough might be on the other side of us stepping out and sharing our story!

~

RECOMMENDED READING

Experiential Storytelling by Mark Miller

Release the Power of Jesus by Bill Johnson

19

STEWARDING TESTIMONY BUILDS A FAITH CULTURE

~~

*Know today that I do not speak with your children,
who have not known and who have not seen the
chastening of the Lord your God, His greatness and
His mighty hand and His outstretched arm—His signs
and His acts which He did in the midst of Egypt, to
Pharaoh king of Egypt, and to all his land; what He
did to the army of Egypt, to their horses and their
chariots: how He made the waters of the Red Sea
overflow them as they pursued you, and how the Lord
has destroyed them to this day; what He did for you in
the wilderness until you came to this place; and what
He did to Dathan and Abiram the sons of Eliab, the
son of Reuben: how the earth opened its mouth and
swallowed them up, their households, their tents, and all
the substance that was in their possession, in the midst
of all Israel—but your eyes have seen every great act
of the Lord which He did. —*DEUTERONOMY 11:2-7

In this final chapter on testimony we will discover how to *sustain* the very source that ignited breakthrough faith in the four friends of the paralytic man. Many Christians have experienced seasons of breakthrough. This is certainly worth celebrating. However, *there is more* we were created to experience! My goal is to stir us up to pursue a lifestyle of breakthrough faith. A vital key to sustaining this supernatural lifestyle is stewarding the testimony of what God has done in our midst.

WE ARE CALLED TO STEWARD GOD'S SUPERNATURAL STORIES

Deuteronomy 11:2-7 reveals a powerful principle in regard to shaping future generations through sharing testimony. Our eyes have been privileged to see supernatural things that future generations have not seen *yet*. What we see and what we experience is our responsibility. When we experience the miraculous, it becomes our realm of stewardship. If we want the eyes of future generations to see the greater works and glory of God manifest on earth, then we need to understand that we are the catalyst for transmitting the testimony of God from one generation to the next. Our stories feed and ignite others' faith.

One of the saddest places to visit is a church or faith community where testimony is not being passed on to the next generation. I know of a few places where the pastors and leaders have experienced a powerful move of God in the past—signs, wonders, healings, and deliverances—everything that was normal in the Book of Acts these leaders enjoyed. The problem is that their stories stopped with them because they failed to pass them on to the next generation.

We cannot let our latter years be spent preparing to voyage off into the glory sunset. Many churches and ministries with older leaders tend to believe this insidious lie of the devil: "You're done. Your time has passed. You're not cool, hip, or relevant. Those kids don't want to listen to you." This is a terrible deception, for the enemy is well aware of the faith that is released when generations connect and align. The stories of one generation have the ability to light the fire of expectancy for the next. Our testimonies are what the young people of this generation *truly* need and *desperately* hunger for.

People and places that have experienced revival in the past have often not seen it sustained for very long. One of the reasons for this is that the move of God distracts us from creating a culture of sustained breakthrough. The very thing we cry out for and desire more than anything else—a supernatural release of God's power and Presence—can actually sidetrack us from implementing the purpose of the outpouring. God's goal for revival has never been to release "sovereign" demonstrations of power that end up going down in history books, but are not sustained from generation to generation. Revival is to be enjoyed, for sure. Renewal brings great refreshing. But in every revival, renewal, and outpouring, there is a divine summons for cultural alignment. How we do life and how we approach church must shift because of the move of God. If it does not, we did not appropriately respond to the divine summons. God is inviting each one of us to adjust the way we see and do life so we can come into greater agreement with Him.

Every sign, every wonder, and every breakthrough must be our invitation to ask, "Father, what do these things say about *You*? How do we adapt and adjust church to what *You* are doing and how *You* are moving in the earth?" Revival testimonies are not intended to simply be cataloged in books; they call us to reevaluate the state of life and the condition of the church. They call us to seek out areas where divine alignment needs to take place.

The stories of one generation have the ability to light the fire of expectancy for the next.

Revival "putters out" not because it is God's sovereign will for it to do so. Revival dies because God was calling a people to embrace a new wineskin. He patiently waits for an individual or a church to get His cue and reorient life to align with Heaven. The problem is that many of us want both. We want the refreshment of the new wine but are comfortable maintaining the old wineskin. Again, this is why revival does not sustain generation after generation. We love the refreshment His Presence and power brings. However, revival also brings death. Death to old systems. Death to old ways. Death to former things. Death to the familiar. Death to our agendas. Death to idols. Death to the way it has always been done before.

Instead, people try to cram the new work of the Holy Spirit into an existing paradigm, program, or protocol. This will never work, and, invariably, a culture of continuous, demonstrated breakthrough faith ceases. In order for us to sustain a lifestyle of breakthrough faith where revival is the norm and not the exception, we must reorient our lives and our churches to embrace testimony as significant.

Testimony is all about shifting culture. This is why God is intent on building a culture of testimony. In every testimony of what God has done or is doing we catch a clearer glimpse of His ways. This is our standard for how to conduct everything in life and church matters—the *ways* of God. Rather than being known as a place of teaching, instruction, and community, I want the church of Jesus Christ to once again be a force on the earth for family, love, and supernatural power. I long for her church to be a community where the ways of the Father are actually made visible to the earth through His people.

Testimony is a key emphasis that the Holy Spirit has been trying to incorporate into standard church practice during every revival that has taken place since the early church. It seems, however, that we continue to lose the memo and go on with business as usual. In the few pages to come, I want to share about the need for creating a culture of testimony in our lives, our homes, and our churches, as well as give some practical ways we can share our testimony and participate in this cultural revolution. New culture is created when individuals come together and commit to transform the culture that presently *is*.

WHY DO WE NEED A CULTURE OF TESTIMONY?

Charles Spurgeon, who is widely regarded as the prince of preachers, delivered a powerful sermon about the desperate need to share the mighty acts of God. His main text was Psalm 44:1: *"We have heard with our ears, O God; our fathers have told us [what] work You did in their days, in the days of old"* (AMP).

When we look back at Israel, the early church, and Christianity up until the last few centuries, testimony was a centerpiece of life and culture. It is safe to say that their culture revolved around testimonies and stories. Testimonies are designed to be "preserved, rehearsed, kept honest, and discussed in conversation."[60] Before I go into the practicality of *how* to build this culture, I want us to consider some of Spurgeon's prophetic observations about how believers throughout history sustained a supernatural culture of testimony, stewarding stories of God's mighty acts from generation to generation. He said:

> Now, among the early Christians and the old believers in the far-off times, nursery tales were far different from what they are now, and the stories with which their children were amused were of a far different class from those which fascinated us in the days of our babyhood.
>
> No doubt, Abraham would talk to young children about the flood, and tell them how the waters overspread the earth, and how Noah alone was saved in the ark. The ancient Israelites, when they dwelt in their own land, would all of them tell their children about the Red Sea, and the plagues which God wrought in Egypt when he brought His people out of the house of bondage.
>
> Among the early Christians we know that it was the custom of parents to recount to their children everything concerning the life of Christ, the acts of the apostles, and the like interesting narratives.
>
> Nay, among our puritanic ancestors such were the stories that regaled. Sitting down by the fireside, before those old Dutch tiles with the quaint eccentric drawings upon them of the history of Christ, mothers would teach their children about

Jesus walking on the water, or of His multiplying the loaves of bread, or of His marvelous transfiguration, or of the crucifixion of Jesus.

Oh, how I would that the like were the tales of the present age, that the stories of our childhood would be again the stories of Christ, and that we would each of us believe that, after all, there can be nothing so interesting as that which is true, and nothing more striking than those stories which are written in sacred writ; nothing that can more truly move the heart of a child than the marvelous works of God which He did in the olden times. It seems that the psalmist who wrote this most musical ode had heard from his father, handed to him by tradition, the stories of the wondrous things which God had done in his day; and afterwards, this sweet singer in Israel taught it to his children, and so was one generation after another led to call God blessed, remembering his mighty acts.[61]

This is Deuteronomy 11:2-7 in action. One generation recognized the importance of what their eyes saw and ensured that the next generation—who did not directly see what God had done—*heard about it.* This builds and sustains a culture of expectant faith.

Pastor Bill Johnson explains that "keeping the testimony means that I diligently preserve the record of what God has done in the past until it becomes the lens through which I see present circumstances."[62] Not only does testimony sustain us personally and give us a God-confidence going into our present circumstances, but it also has the power to give others supernatural confidence, empowering them to stare impossibilities in the face and know that the same God *who moved* in the past for us will *move again* for them.

God's will is not a cycle of victory, defeat, victory, defeat, defeat, seasonal victory, etc. Victory should be the normal expression of the Christian life. Victory is not insulation from problems; rather, victory is breakthrough faith expressed in *every* season of life. And how is this faith sustained? Its root is not in a principle or formula; breakthrough faith remains constant because the object of our faith remains constant. Our faith is in a Person. The wonderful thing about a culture of testimony is that by being immersed in stories of how this faithful person has come through, time after time after time, we are reminded of who He is in even greater ways.

KEYS TO BUILDING A CULTURE OF TESTIMONY

In Spurgeon's sermon, he recognized the missing ingredient in contemporary church culture—*the power of testimony*. He concluded his introduction by giving a very clear reason *why* it is so important for us to share the mighty acts of God with the next generation and *how* we can start doing this on a regular basis:

> My aim and object will be to *excite your minds to seek after the like*; that looking back upon what God has done, you may be induced to look forward with the eye of expectation, hoping that He will again stretch forth His potent hand and His holy arm, and repeat those mighty acts He performed in ancient days.[63]

Victory is not insulation from problems; rather, victory is breakthrough faith expressed in *every* season of life.

Here is what Spurgeon proposes that a culture of storytelling will do for us, our family, and our church:

Exciting our minds to seek after the like: When we share testimony of God's supernatural power through story, we excite people's minds to entertain new possibilities of what God can and will do for them. As they hear about miraculous things God has done in times past or that He is doing today, their faith is stirred up to believe for the same supernatural results in their lives.

Looking back positions us to look forward: For those of you who are older in the faith and have seen your share of God's power, miracles, and acts—do not be silent. Do not go off quietly into the sunset without passing on to the next generation what you've seen God do. On your way to Heaven, you can actually stir up a new generation to access and experience the power of Heaven on earth. Spurgeon explained that by recounting what God has accomplished in the past, we release an attitude of expectation for the same God to perform the same works *again*.

Do not be afraid or timid about mentoring young people. Take them into your homes and into your offices. Have small groups with them. Go to Starbucks. It does not matter what it looks like. Simply steward your testimony by telling a new generation about what your eyes have seen God do. They do not want anecdotes. Sermons are okay, but they are not enough to fuel their passion. You have something that a generation craves. You can make the final era of your life incredibly fruitful by recognizing the power of *looking forward* beyond yourself—your generation, your church, or your ministry—and sowing into an entire generation who will actually see the glory of God manifested on earth.

One Scripture I can never escape from is in Psalm 90:16: *"Let Your work appear to Your servants, and Your glory to their children."* You have experienced the mighty works of God, not just for dazzle, show, or spectacle. You have not experienced them even just for personal breakthrough, blessing, or betterment. You have a responsibility to sow into the next generation by sharing the testimonies of what your eyes have seen the living God do. This causes their hearts to *burn* to step into their inheritance: the manifestation of God's glory in the earth through His people. What does this mean? A generation well fed on the works of God will actually walk in the supernatural as a sustained lifestyle. As an entire generation presses in to access everything Jesus died to give them and everything Pentecost made available, Numbers 14:21 will surely come to pass: *"all the earth shall be filled with the glory of the Lord."*

Two modern examples that immediately come to my mind are Karen Wheaton and Reinhard Bonnke. Karen Wheaton was a very successful recording artist in Christian music. However, God clearly called her back to her hometown of Hamilton, Alabama, to start a youth center.

She proceeded to argue with God, informing Him why she was the least likely candidate for the job. She did not consider herself cool or hip. She did not dress, act, or look like other youth leaders. She was not up to date on all the latest youth gimmicks. And yet, the one thing she knew is what defines her ministry, The Ramp, to this very day. She knew the way into the Presence of God and how to bring the kids with her. Because of this, The Ramp has been experiencing sustained revival for over a decade, with thousands of kids coming through those doors every single year, being radically marked by the Presence and power of God. The Ramp does not simply produce converts; it raises up and sends out revivalists.

Reinhard Bonnke is a German-born evangelist who has conducted history-making Gospel crusades throughout the continent of Africa. Tens of millions have come to know Jesus Christ under his ministry. Bonnke is currently in his seventies, showing no signs of slowing down. Not only has the Lord impressed upon him to launch a series of Gospel crusades throughout the United States, but he has been intentionally connecting with the next generation by speaking at youth/young adult events and conferences (The Ramp, Jesus Culture, etc.).

Remember—on your way to Heaven, you can actually stir up a new generation to access and experience the power of Heaven on earth.

Leaders like Bonnke illustrate the point of this chapter. When he tells stories of what he has seen God do during his time here on earth, the fire upon his testimony becomes a catalyst that launches a new generation into a radical lifestyle of breakthrough faith. Bonnke always makes it very clear that the same Holy Spirit who anointed him lives inside every single believer, empowering and enabling them to flow in the same mighty works. In fact, one of the most inspiring works of testimony you can read is Bonnke's autobiography, *Living a Life of Fire*. I am so grateful for generals like Bonnke and Wheaton who are giving the next season of their lives to building this culture of testimony in a whole new generation.

Repeating the Mighty Acts of God in Our Day: Making reference to this subject, Bill Johnson explains, "The stories of God's intervention set a legal precedent for the miraculous. They establish an understanding of God's nature and His heart and provide the ongoing element to the miraculous."[64] The key is *expectation*. Spurgeon put it this way, "'Well,' says one, 'but I do not expect to see any great things.' Then, my dear friend, you will not be disappointed, for you will not see them; but those that expect them *shall* see them."[65]

We need to be a people filled with expectation once again. Hope—as defined by Scripture—is all about expectation, not merely wishing or wondering. There is a confident expectation that God *will* do what He *has done*.

Keys to Building a Culture of Testimony

Finally, I want to share some very practical ways that all of us can begin to build a culture of testimony, both individually and corporately.

Make testimony a priority, and not a side issue. Testimony must become as foundational to our services and lives as the Word of God, worship, integrity, developing the character of Christ, and the gifts of the Spirit. Before we experience the fruit of testimony, we must understand its priority and importance in our daily lives.

Make time for testimony. In our small groups, Sunday schools, church services, and events, we must set apart time for people to give testimony of what God *has done* in their lives. If we consider testimony important, then we will make it part of our church services and everyday lives. We should *always* be ready to share our stories, from our testimony of salvation to our story of healing, freedom, deliverance, family restoration, marriage miracle, etc. Testimony is not just about our salvation experience; it is *any* story of God moving in our lives.

Try out a testimony service. For some, this may sound "old school," but come on—give it a go! The church in this generation is *not* lacking in innovation and creativity. We have what it takes to bring testimony back to the Kingdom and see the power of God released in incredible ways. In fact, people are often more inclined to hear stories over sermons. Just be sure that the stories celebrate the supernatural acts of God and ultimately unveil the nature of God as revealed in Scripture.

SOME PRACTICAL WAYS TO SHARE OUR TESTIMONY

In closing, here are some everyday ways each one of us can personally share our testimony. I am totally aware that not everyone is a public speaker, pastor, or preacher. This is why there are so many different storytelling options available. I am certain there is at least one tool that each of us can use to declare the mighty acts that God has done in our lives, and, in turn, stir up breakthrough faith in others.

For preachers, preach about *your testimony*. Share about how God has supernaturally transformed *your* life and tell stories of how you have seen God supernaturally move in others' lives.

For writers, write about it.

If you are into social media, Tweet and Facebook about the supernatural things God is doing in your life. This gives you an amazing platform to constantly be sharing what God is doing with countless people.

If you have a blog, blog about it.

If you have a strong video presence, Vlog about it (Video Blog), do a Google Hangout, record YouTube videos, or start a YouTube Channel, etc.

If you have a strong radio voice or persona, create a free radio show on BlogTalk Radio.

The technology (most of it is free) available today is absolutely stunning! If you have a platform of *any* kind, use it to share testimony of what God has done and is doing in your life, or the things you have witnessed God do for others. When this becomes standard practice for the body of Christ, and stories of God's compassion, greatness, and supernatural power become everyday vocabulary for us, breakthrough faith will become the norm, not the exception.

POINT OF BREAKTHROUGH

Faith to release the power of God is sustained through building a culture of testimony. This takes place when the stories of

God's miracles and wonders are passed down generationally.
Instead of simply becoming memorialized or celebrated,
the testimonies of God's mighty works actually transform
the way people see God, interact with Him, and, in turn,
walk out their Christian lives on an everyday basis.

~~~

RECOMMENDED READING

The Essential Guide to Healing
by Bill Johnson and Randy Clark

Living a Life of Fire by Reinhard Bonnke

"The Story of God's Mighty Acts"
sermon by Charles Spurgeon[66]

PRESENCE

~~~

...He was in the house. —MARK 2:1

20

PRESENCE INCREASES OUR FAITH-AWARENESS

~~

For you are the temple of the living God. As
God has said: "I will dwell in them and walk
among them. I will be their God, and they shall
be My people." —2 CORINTHIANS 6:16

This is a *very* special chapter to me. The truth we are discussing here is the very reality that beautifully changed my life back in July of 1999 and has been powerfully transforming it ever since. It was my encounter in God's Presence that shifted *my entire life* in a single moment—and it has only been in recent years that I started to understand why this experience was so transformative.

When we understand that the God who is infinitely able and lovingly willing lives *within us*, awareness of faith skyrockets. It is one thing to believe we have inherited breakthrough faith because of the cross. We might believe that we possess it but have difficulty believing that we have the power to put it to work in our everyday lives. God made provision for this too! God gave us both an inheritance *and* the power to put that inheritance to work. The purchase of Calvary made faith possible, but it is the power of Pentecost that equips us to walk out a supernatural lifestyle of breakthrough faith.

GOD CHANGES ADDRESSES

The inheritance of the Holy Spirit living within us is both mind-blowing and revolutionary. Consider the apostle Paul's prayer in Ephesians 1:17-18: *"that the God of our Lord Jesus Christ, the Father of glory, may give to you the spirit of wisdom and revelation in the knowledge of Him, the eyes of your understanding being enlightened; that you may know what is the hope of His calling, what are the riches of the glory of His inheritance in the saints."*

Paul's language at the end of these verses is extraordinary. Where is this glory of His inheritance? It dwells within the saints. There is a priceless inheritance living on the inside of each one of us just waiting for us to make a withdrawal.

The problem is that many people do not live consistently awed by this reality because they do not possess the vision that Paul is presenting here. This is the ground we are going to be covering in the pages ahead. We are going on a very strategic journey, tracking the movement of God's Presence throughout the ages, which ultimately culminated in His present-day address.

In Mark's Gospel Jesus came to a physical house. We clearly see that Jesus was in the house. It was in this context where He preached, ministered, and ultimately healed the paralytic who was lowered through the ceiling. We also see that it was in this environment that the *"power of the Lord was present to heal"* (Luke 5:17). Everyone crammed into a physical place where Jesus was because, at the time, Jesus was one man with physical limitations. Make no mistake about it, Jesus was 100 percent God but He was also a man anointed by the Holy Spirit.

> **The purchase of Calvary made faith possible, but it is the power of Pentecost that equips us to walk out a supernatural lifestyle of breakthrough faith.**

At this point in history, the Old Covenant had not yet concluded, which meant that the abiding Presence of the Holy Spirit could *only* rest upon Jesus because Jesus was the only One without sin and thus compatible with the Presence of God. Before the Spirit could actually live inside of every believer, Jesus' blood had to be shed for the complete payment for our sin. That took place at the cross.

Things have dramatically shifted since the era when the paralyzed man was lowered through the ceiling. While Mark 2 is an outstanding example of breakthrough faith, the Holy Spirit has upgraded the experience that is available for all believers. No longer is it required for people to cram into a house where Jesus is physically present to experience His power. Because of the cross, Jesus is no longer restricted to a tabernacle, temple, or single human body. He is currently seated at the Father's right hand in Heaven (see Acts 2:33).

On the Day of Pentecost, God released the Holy Spirit into the earth. It is the indwelling presence of the Holy Spirit *within every believer* that makes it possible for every single person we come into contact with to have an encounter with God. Under the New Covenant, because of Jesus' blood, *each of us are now the house* where God's Presence is present to heal and transform.

You house the Presence of God that charges the atmosphere with Heaven's miracle-working ability.

You house the power that turns impossible situations around and releases Kingdom solutions.

You house the Person of the Holy Spirit who makes every miracle, sign, and wonder possible—and ultimately uses these miracles to point everyone to their supernatural source, Jesus Christ.

One of the first things we did in this book was focus on the foundational topic of the knowledge of God. Why? Because when our lifelong quest is after the Person of God, and God alone, then our vision of who actually lives inside of us increases. In order to know who we are and what we offer to the world, it is essential for us to first experience intimacy with God. When we know who He is, we know exactly who we carry inside of us. In turn, we then discover what He is capable of doing through us.

God is what we offer to this world. Any human being, sinner or saint, can offer good deeds, philanthropy, and charity to the world. These are all noble causes, but when charged with the power of Pentecost that each of us carries, the solution released through us is nothing short of supernatural. In fact, it is the *only* solution that satisfies the void inside every human heart. I pray that our spiritual eyes would be increasingly enlightened to the Precious One that we host with our lives!

> **Because of the cross, Jesus is no longer restricted to a tabernacle, temple, or single human body.**

There is nothing any of us can do to make God any larger than He already is. He is truly bigger than our ability to mentally comprehend or fathom. As we make the character, nature, and very Person of God our lifelong pursuit, then day after day we will step into a greater revelation of who this great God is. The result is that breakthrough faith will be activated within us. When we behold God for who He is and then marry that revelation with the fact that this great God, through the Person of the Holy Spirit, actually lives inside of us, then we come to one logical conclusion: nothing is impossible. It is no longer some Christian jargon or feel-good platitude. No, seriously. *Nothing* is impossible. Let it actually sink in: God lives inside of us and He is summoning us to be overwhelmed by this incredible reality, which is often taken for granted.

It sounds like A.W. Tozer was grappling with this extraordinary truth as he wrote,

> There is an unseen Deity present, a knowing, feeling Personality, and He is indivisible from the Father and the Son, so that if you were to be suddenly transferred to Heaven itself you wouldn't be any closer to God than you are now, for God is already here. Changing your geographical location would not bring you any nearer to God nor God any nearer to you,

because the indivisible Trinity is present, and all that the Son is the Holy Ghost is, and all that the Father is the Holy Ghost is, and the Holy Ghost is in His Church.[67]

What would it look like if the body of Christ *actually believed it was indwelt by God?* What if we started to agree with the fact that we have a glorious inheritance living on the inside of us—the Spirit of God, who is no more or no less than the Father and the Son? We would change the world, there is no question about it.

Before we practically apply the reality of God's indwelling Presence to our daily lives, it is important to have a basic understanding of the precious jewel we have received in the Holy Spirit. Truly, our faith ancestors and forerunners of old could have only dreamed about the age you and I are living in—the day where all believers have unrestricted access to the Presence that they so deeply cherished and revered.

THE JOURNEY OF GOD'S PRESENCE

Let us briefly review the journey of God's Presence, from Eden to the church. This timeline reveals God's original intent, and how, because of Jesus' blood, what was often considered to be the benchmark of Old Testament supernatural experience has been significantly upgraded for us today. The question remains, Do we actually believe it?

Eden

In Genesis there is an indication that God walked *with* mankind. When Adam and Eve sinned, Scripture tells us that they *"hid themselves from the presence of the Lord God among the trees of the garden"* (Gen. 3:8). In Eden God walked among men. So many of us think that if we could "only go back to Eden, that would be amazing!" Do not memorialize Eden. In it we see a glimpse of God's original intent, but I have exciting news for you: Christ Jesus was the walking, talking expression of the Father's original intent. And because of Jesus' redemptive work on the cross, something *greater* than Eden has become available.

223

Tabernacle

The tabernacle represents the heart of God to dwell *among* His people, though sinful and rebellious (see Exod. 29:45-46). The tabernacle is a prophetic picture of what Jesus would make available to us through His work on the cross. Another phrase assigned to the tabernacle was the tent of meeting (see Exod. 39:32). In other words, it was the *tent of encounter*. God met with Moses, His friend, in this place. Because of Jesus, a day would come when all believers would be identified as friends of God (see John 15:15) and would be invited into His glorious Presence through the work of Calvary (see Heb. 10:19-22). The tabernacle was also mobile, a prophetic image of a people who would one day house the Presence and carry God from place to place.

Temple

Much could be written about the temple of Solomon, but for the purpose of our journey here I want to study the tension concerning this building project. The temple was really David's idea. Being a lover of God's Presence, King David considered the fact that he was living in opulent and blessed living quarters while the Ark of the Covenant, housing the very Presence of God, *"dwells inside tent curtains"* (2 Sam. 7:2). Such living conditions were not sufficient for David. So he proposed a building project—the temple of the Lord. Even though it was absolutely stunning (Solomon ended up overseeing its construction), one can sense by reading Second Samuel 7:5-16 that God had something greater in store. God spoke to King David through Nathan the prophet, saying:

> *When your days are fulfilled and you rest with your fathers, I will set up your seed after you, who will come from your body, and I will establish his kingdom. He shall build a house for My name, and I will establish the throne of his kingdom forever* (2 Samuel 7:12-13).

Even though David's natural seed—Solomon—built a physical house called the temple, God had something significantly *greater* in mind.

Because of Jesus' redemptive work on the cross, something *greater* than Eden has become available.

Jesus

The Son of God was also called the Son of David. In other words, the One who was completely God was also 100 percent human. Only God could pull that one off. Think about it for a moment—God dwelling inside of God. It happened! God maintained His identity as God but lived completely as a man who was anointed by the same Holy Spirit that we have received. This is significant, for the Man Christ Jesus became the model and example for the temple that God the Father had envisioned back in 2 Samuel 7:12-13. Bricks and mortar were never God's idea for housing His Presence.

Jesus the Messiah shed His blood so that the example of Jesus the Man could be followed by every single born-again believer throughout history. Jesus modeled a temple of God constructed by flesh and bone—a human being who housed God's Presence. Nothing like this had *ever* been experienced before in history, even with Adam and Eve. God *walked* with man in Eden, yes. God *talked* with man, for sure. In different instances, God even *used* man, clothing mortal flesh with power and ability and might for a season to accomplish certain tasks. But God *living inside of man*, making humanity His dwelling place, was completely off the grid. Jesus inaugurated the most revolutionary reality conceivable.

Consider part of Stephen's final sermon before he was stoned to death:

> *David found favor in God's sight, and asked that he might find a dwelling place for the God of Jacob. But it was Solomon who built a house for Him. However, the Most High does not dwell in houses made by human hands* (Acts 7:46-48 NASB).

The power of Jesus' blood made it possible for you and I—a people of flesh and blood—to house the eternal God. Let this sink in for a moment. *This is the reality greater than Eden.* Talk about a breeding ground for breakthrough faith! Under the Old Covenant, people dropped dead when they approached God's manifest Presence incorrectly. Now, the Presence of the King of Glory lives inside of you and inside of me. We are the only structure God ever willed to carry His Presence.

God's excitement about us becoming His house is revealed when the *"curtain of the temple was torn in two, from top to bottom"* the day Jesus was crucified (Mark 15:38 ESV). The born-again believer has been designed in such a way that he or she is actually capable of housing the supernatural presence of God. This should supercharge our thanksgiving and appreciation for the priceless gift of God's Holy Spirit.

> **Jesus the Messiah shed His blood so that the example of Jesus the Man could be followed by every single born-again believer throughout history.**

Pentecost

And finally, the Day of Pentecost made it possible for every single believer to partake of what Jesus received in Mark 1:9-10 at His baptism: *"In those days Jesus came from Nazareth of Galilee and was baptized by John in the Jordan. And when He came up out of the water, immediately he saw the heavens being torn open and the Spirit descending on Him like a dove"* (ESV).

Jesus' baptism tore open the Heavens, Jesus' blood kept the Heavens open, and Pentecost ensured that the Heavens would remain open over us. When we came to Christ, we inherited the power of Pentecost. God came to live inside of us, which means that Heaven is currently open over our lives in the same way that it was open over Jesus' life. I love how Sam Storms expresses this overwhelming reality: "We are now the Temple of God! If the inanimate structure of the old covenant trembled and shook at God's presence, what is our response, we in whom this same glorious and holy God now lives?"[68]

Jesus' baptism tore open the Heavens, Jesus' blood kept the Heavens open, and Pentecost ensured that the Heavens would remain open over us.

MY BAPTISM OF FIRE, YOUR INVITATION TO BREAKTHROUGH FAITH

A.W. Tozer once said, "We can press our way into the sanctuary of the holy of holies, and with our hearts, we can meet, know, feel, sense and experience God in a manner more wonderful than any man or woman can experience any human being."[69] One encounter in God's Presence is enough to awaken breakthrough faith that can completely change the trajectory of our lives. I call this a baptism of fire. Many have experienced the baptism of the Holy Spirit, and I truly celebrate that doctrine. However, there are many who have embraced a doctrine without having an encounter. I pray that my story will be your invitation to press in for such an encounter.

As previously mentioned, I attended a "faith church" for a little over seven years. Some of the principles I was taught were beneficial; some were completely imbalanced. When the bent was toward materialism and using almighty God as a cosmic vending machine to fulfill our every whim, things got severely off track. Prosperity and success became elevated above humility and love.

However, my passion for the impossible never shifted—never waned. I desperately tried to throw out all of the "faith stuff"—believe me. But there were certain things I could not let go of because something inside me would not allow it. I know now that this "something" was a Someone—the Holy Spirit Himself. After leaving that church and visiting other (vastly different) churches that did not agree with any of the supernatural beliefs I upheld, there was still a fire burning within me to walk in breakthrough faith and see God's supernatural power invade impossible situations. I soon discovered that I was not possessed by principles. I was not some by-product of the church I attended. I was not a parrot of the "faith" teachers or spiritual superstars I was exposed to in those circles. My anchor was the encounter I had with God before I was ever introduced to distorted faith doctrine.

That one moment, though not naturally spectacular, made me aware that the Presence of God was real. I was touched so deeply and so profoundly that to this day I passionately long to give my life to continuing the journey that began back in July of 1999. At the time, the Holy Spirit had me on a God-quest. I was sixteen years old, a recent recipient of my driver's license, and visiting different churches, exploring what each one had to offer. Curiosity brought me to a local non-denominational church. It was definitely different from what I had experienced up to that point in my life. Contemporary worship. People raising their hands, clapping, and worshipping God with excitement. It seemed a little far out and (quite honestly) creepy to me. In fact, I would often arrive at service *after* the music had concluded—until that glorious night in July 1999.

It was a Saturday night service. I actually made it in time for the worship set, and while I stood there during one of the songs, I tangibly felt the Spirit of God touch my hands like light electricity, and then touch my heart like a gentle, warm heat. No, I did not fall on the ground and have a dramatic experience—although I have had some of those since. What I tasted of God's Presence in that moment was strong enough to convince me that He was real, He was near, and that He was worthy of my entire life.

We should never confuse the dramatic with the Presence of God. For some people, it can be like sticking their fingers into an electrical outlet—and they actually *look and act* like they are being shocked. For some, however, the encounter goes practically unseen on the outside. But something life-changing takes place on the inside of the person. God's Presence comes subtly but strongly. It is carried on a word spoken, on a message we hear that causes our hearts to burn, or during worship, a missions trip, or even while driving in our car. God is no respecter of persons and He is likewise no respecter of methods. His wind will blow how He wills.

These touches of His Presence and fresh baptisms of fire can happen anywhere, anytime. I encourage you to invite them and welcome them. Even though we pursue God and not experiences, we serve a God who has a powerful track record for touching His people in the place of encounter. The result of these experiences in God's Presence is radical breakthrough faith. History reveals that such faith releases entire nations from captivity, causes the sun to stand still, defeats entire armies with only 300 men, calls fire down from Heaven, and births a church that turns the world upside down. All of this is birthed in the place of God's Presence, where man collided with the divine.

POINT OF BREAKTHROUGH

God never meant for His powerful Presence to reside in a building or tent—our body is the only structure ever designed to sufficiently house God. Because of Jesus' redemptive work on the cross and the outpouring of the Holy Spirit at Pentecost, this reality is now available to every single believer, including you!

RECOMMENDED READING

Man: The Dwelling Place of God by A.W. Tozer

Experiencing the Presence of God by A.W. Tozer

Drawing Near and *A Heart Ablaze* by John Bevere

Manifest Presence by Jack Hayford

Hosting the Presence by Bill Johnson

21

PRESENCE IS THE GATEWAY INTO GREATER WORKS

~~

Now to Him who is able to do exceedingly abundantly above all that we ask or think, according to the power that works in us. —EPHESIANS 3:20

This chapter has been written to blow your mind and whet your spiritual appetite like never before. God is summoning His people to get radical. The Holy Spirit is inviting the body of Christ to start pressing in to experience realities that we have only read or heard about, but have not personally experienced...*yet*. Just because we have not yet experienced something does not mean the reality of it is unavailable or inaccessible to us. We may have never gone to Paris, but that does not mean Paris is off-limits. Just because we have not been to Paris does not mean we cannot go to Paris. In the same way, just because we have not experienced some of the supernatural activity we read about in Scripture does not mean that such realities are off-limits. If anything, the lifestyle that Jesus modeled should become our normal, and what Jesus invited us into should become our great pursuit.

God lives inside of you. That is *incredible* in and of itself! Such a truth is so awe-inspiring that we could literally pack up and go home on that revelation alone. But isn't it just like our abundantly generous Father to offer us even *more*. In these final chapters together, I pray that the Holy Spirit comes and absolutely ruins us for any form of Christianity that is moderate or mundane. I pray that the Holy Spirit deposits an insatiable craving in our spirits that never leaves.

Yes, we have talked about the supernatural, miracle-working ability of breakthrough faith. But we must remember, breakthrough faith comes from God alone. It is His gift. If this faith comes from God, then there are absolutely no limits to what it can accomplish. It is *His* faith. He spoke into nothingness and creation happened. We carry and steward the faith of *that* God—the Genesis 1:1 God. Is *anything* impossible or off-limits to those who possess this supernatural, breakthrough faith?

Jesus modeled a "normal" supernatural lifestyle that we can all walk in. He healed the sick, cast out demons, set captives free, raised the dead, and turned impossible situations around. *He* is the author and finisher of our faith (see Heb. 12:2). If *the same Jesus* who performed the miraculous works that we read about in the Gospels is indeed the One who authored our faith, then our faith should be able to do everything He did. It contains His very DNA. What we received at salvation was a supernatural faith capable of accessing every reality that we read about in Scripture and see modeled in the life of Jesus Christ.

I pray that by this point in the book you recognize the availability and accessibility of supernatural Christianity. Now it is time to take it a step further and discover what should become the next frontier of our pursuit—*the greater works*.

> The lifestyle that Jesus modeled should become our normal, and what Jesus invited us into should become our great pursuit.

OUR INVITATION TO PURSUE GREATER WORKS

Too many believers are coasting on yesterday (how they have always known and done Christianity), when in fact Jesus made realities available to us that are more than our mortal minds can possibly comprehend. One of the mind-blowing realities that Jesus presented to us is the often misunderstood or watered-down concept of "greater works." If break-through faith is really the faith of God living inside of us, then it goes without saying that this faith is more than sufficient to equip us to do everything that Jesus said we would be able to do.

> *Most assuredly, I say to you, he who believes in Me, the works that I do he will do also; and greater works than these he will do, because I go to My Father* (John 14:12).

This is one of those scary and intimidating statements in Scripture that we either ignore or reduce to the conceivable. We either ignore it all together or we redefine what "greater works" are in a way that our natural minds can process more comfortably. I just performed an Internet search on "greater works quotes" and was amazed at how many articles were dedicated to explaining away what greater works *really* mean. Lazy theology takes a supernatural concept and endeavors to rationalize it down to a level that the unrenewed, carnal mind can easily process and the natural man can comfortably implement. I don't know about you, but I don't want that. I do not want to bring God's standard of living down to my level. Quite the opposite, in fact. I want to raise my standard to come into agreement with His.

So what are we to do with John 14:12? One approach, as mentioned above, is to redefine what sounds impossible and reduce it to what is accomplishable with our human efforts. In this perspective, "greater works" simply refers to the "scope" of ministry impact, because the Holy Spirit now lives inside of every believer and is no longer restricted to Jesus alone. This is pretty impressive in and of itself, if we think about it. Because of the Holy Spirit, millions of people across the earth are invited into a supernatural lifestyle where it becomes biblically legal for them to desire miracles in greater size and scope to what Jesus did.

Unfortunately, this is not usually what people who embrace this perspective mean. They simply maintain that "greater works" refers to *more* philanthropic, humanitarian exploits that are performed in Jesus' name. We must always celebrate those who meet practical needs, as this is an essential component of the Christian life. At the same time, it is a travesty to our spiritual inheritance to redefine greater works as that which can be accomplished by any human being apart from the power of God, be it an entrepreneur or Hollywood actor.

I would *almost* buy into the whole "greater works" redefinition thing *if* it were not for a man named Paul. While there are other noteworthy figures throughout church history who stepped into the realm of greater works, we are all on safe, level ground by briefly examining the apostle Paul's journey into this demonstration. We reviewed his pursuit of closeness with God earlier on as we were studying the importance of the knowledge of God in laying our faith foundation. It is now time for us to revisit this topic and consider the fruit of building on such a foundation.

PAUL: THE MAN WHO PRESSED IN FOR GREATER THINGS

What happens when God becomes our great quest and our mind is consistently stretched by His greatness and vastness? Do we know what positions us to step into the realm of "greater works"? It is when we recognize that the God living inside of us is bigger than our theology can contain or express. When we live awestruck before God's grandeur, then and only then are we standing on the edge of the extraordinary miracles that we see in Acts 19: *"God was performing extraordinary miracles by the hands of Paul, so that handkerchiefs or aprons were even carried from his body to the sick, and the diseases left them and the evil spirits went out"* (Acts 19:11-12 NASB).

Earlier in our journey, we started to look at the correlation between breakthrough faith and the pursuit of the knowledge of God. Acts 19:11-12 is the result of Paul's great quest that is so beautifully expressed in Philippians 3:8: *"Yet indeed I also count all things loss for the excellence of the knowledge of Christ Jesus my Lord."* Paul did not pursue greater levels of faith. Paul was not on the hunt for more spectacular demonstrations of supernatural power. He was not seeking principles, precepts, or practical things to do. He was not looking for the Ten Steps to Get Your Miracle or the Twenty Keys to Access Your Breakthrough. Paul's great quest was to know God the Father through intimacy.

Because of Jesus' blood and because of the Holy Spirit living within us, it is now possible for us to know the Father intimately. Jesus stated clearly in John 14:12 that greater works were possible *"because I go to My Father."* By Jesus going to the Father, it became possible for the mighty Presence dwelling inside the Son of God to take up residence in the sons of men. This opened the door to a reality where anointed men and women throughout the ages would become filled with God and do the works of Jesus on earth.

> **When we live awestruck before God's grandeur, then and only then are we standing on the edge of the extraordinary miracles.**

Even though Jesus performed many signs and wonders, it almost seemed like there were some He was reserving for us, the redeemed bride of Christ, to release through fellowship and intimacy with the Holy Spirit. *Extraordinary miracles. Greater works.* That was the great quest Jesus made available through His death on the cross—intimately knowing God, and then representing God by having God live inside of and move through mortal vessels. For centuries that temple veil prevented humanity from engaging this pursuit, the very quest that consumed the apostle Paul. Even Jesus' disciples who walked the planet alongside Him, as amazing as that sounds, were inaccessible to what Paul had, and by extension, to what you and I have—the indwelling Spirit of God. This is absolutely astonishing.

Paul's great prayer continues to stir us to press in for the greater glory, the greater works, the greater miracles, and above all, the greater knowledge of the Glorious One. Reflect on these words from Paul's prayer:

That the God of our Lord Jesus Christ, the Father of glory,
may give to you the spirit of wisdom and revelation in the

knowledge of Him, the eyes of your understanding being enlightened; that you may know what is the hope of His calling, what are the riches of the glory of His inheritance in the saints (Ephesians 1:17-18).

Paul recognized that there was an inheritance inside of us, which in order to understand and access, we would require supernatural wisdom and revelation. This inheritance is none other than the powerful Presence of the Holy Spirit. He is the One who makes breakthrough faith a reality in our lives.

PAUL: THE MAN SATURATED IN GOD'S PRESENCE

Paul also wrote, *"For you are the temple of the living God"* (2 Cor. 6:16). This passage tells us exactly *where* the glorious inheritance is— *inside of every believer.* As Paul pursued the knowledge of God, he also simultaneously sought understanding of how to steward the Presence of the Eternal One that dwelt inside of him. Do we really get this? If we did, I am convinced that every single believer would refuse to settle for average Christianity. Even the "normative" miracles, signs, and wonders would not be the finish line.

Jesus introduced the concept of "greater works" in John 14, while Paul demonstrated it in action in Acts 19. There were miracles, and then we see *extraordinary miracles.* This is not license for discontentment and spiritual greed. Remember, we are always satisfied but hungry. Why are we always hungry? It is because there is always more of God to be experienced and released. It is time for us to model Paul, pursue the knowledge of God, and recognize that as we grow in knowledge of who God is, then we will increase in revelation of the One who lives inside of us. This is the key to walking in greater works—how we interact with the One dwelling within, for it is His Presence that we are called to release to the world around us.

This quest is what caused Paul's very garments to carry the Presence and anointing of God. There was such faith in the *Presence upon* Paul that according to Acts 19 pieces of clothing that were on him were placed on those who were diseased and demonized, and they were healed. Sadly, certain people have run with this verse and, in some ways, perverted it: "Call this number right now, make your donation and receive a prayer cloth that God's 'Man of Power for the Hour' prayed over. The bigger the donation, the better the anointing."

Before Acts 19, and then after Acts 19, we do not read *anywhere* of anyone teaching about anointed clothing. Does that deny the Presence of God that saturated Paul's clothes? No. What it shows us is that there is a higher pursuit than miracle-working garments. This is the pursuit of God's presence. When His Presence is our paramount desire, we become saturated. We walk in a lifelong splash zone. It is unavoidable. Paul was a passionate man and, in turn, became a saturated man. He pursued the One who dwelt within, and as a result of that communion with the Holy Spirit, Paul experienced a true from-the-inside-out transformation. He enjoyed such deep fellowship with the Spirit of God that the man's soul was not only transformed but his physical body was impacted.

How is this evidence of greater works? Remember the woman with the blood flow who pressed through the crowd and touched the hem of Jesus' garment (see Mark 5:25-34)? She had to go to where Jesus was. With Paul, the man was so drenched in the Presence of God that people were able to take pieces of cloth and handkerchiefs that were worn on his presence-saturated body and bring these articles to those who needed healing and deliverance. This is a perfect example of a "greater work" that Jesus spoke about.

For some reading this, it may sound offensive to talk about a flesh-and-blood person performing a "greater work" than Jesus. The example is *very offensive* if we think that the mortal human vessel was the one performing the greater work. Controversy is silenced when we quickly refocus on the author of *all* greater works, Jesus Christ Himself. Jesus is still doing the works. Luke introduces the Book of Acts and describes his Gospel account in this manner: *"The former account I made, O Theophilus, of all that Jesus began both to do and teach"* (Acts 1:1). Note the phrase *"of all that Jesus began to do."* Though He is seated at the Father's right hand, His earthly ministry continues through the power of the Holy Spirit living inside of believers. This is what makes it possible for people like you and me to step into the reality of greater works.

When we look at Paul, we catch a glimpse of a man who embraced Jesus' bold invitation and stepped into the "greater works" reality. Paul was not some spiritual superman. Sometimes we inappropriately elevate the apostles to divine status. They were not. If Elijah, who called down fire from Heaven, is described as a person with "like passions" as us (see James 5:17-18), Paul (a former persecutor of the church), Peter (the one who denied Jesus three times), and the rest of the crew were not spiritual supermen with a 2.0, upgraded faith. What they all received, we now possess.

> Controversy is silenced when we quickly refocus on the author of *all* greater works, Jesus Christ.

IT'S LEGAL TO CRY OUT FOR MORE

Paul said to the Corinthians, *"But we all, with unveiled face, beholding as in a mirror the glory of the Lord, are being transformed into the same image from glory to glory, just as by the Spirit of the Lord"* (2 Cor. 3:18). And A.W. Tozer said, "Everything Jesus Christ did for us we can have in this age. Victorious living, joyous living, holy living, fruitful living, wondrous, ravishing knowledge of the Triune God—all of this is ours."[70] Scriptures like Second Corinthians 3:18 and quotes like Tozer's make it spiritually legal for us to press in for more of God. How can we receive more of Someone we received in fullness because of Pentecost? Is there some type of Holy Ghost 2.0 or faith upgrade that we are unaware of?

As with all things in the Christian life, there is a delicate balance to be maintained here. Our pursuit of more is very specific and scriptural. In Second Corinthians 3 Paul reveals that more is the key to more. In other words, the more we behold the Lord, the more we are transformed into the same image, from one degree of glory to the next. There is more glory available to us! There are deeper places in God's Presence that we can explore! There are clearer whispers of His voice! There is greater insight into His Word! There are more dynamic demonstrations of His power! It is not about wanting more of God, as if we need to receive more of Him to come out of Heaven. Pentecost was sufficient.

The God of all glory lives inside of us and Heaven is wide open over our lives. We don't have to beg God for anything, as if there is more of Him that we actually need to receive. Instead, we are pursuing greater agreement between our theology and experience, alignment between what we have *already received* and what Scripture says is available for us to *experience* and *release*. There is so much more, and I pray that after reading this chapter, your hunger is stirred up to experience and release more of what you have already received by exercising your faith.

If there is a modern example of one who walked with God and demonstrated both His love and power, it was Kathryn Kuhlman. This woman who experienced tremendous breakthrough in the realm of healing and miracles was *still* hungry for more. As she was bearing her soul in a revealing sermon to the students at Oral Roberts University, she opened her message by praying, "No one in the whole world is as hungry for *more* than the one who is speaking this morning...every atom of my being is crying out for more. *There is so much more.*"[71] Greater works are available and accessible on the other side of a lifestyle that presses in for more. Get ready!

POINT OF BREAKTHROUGH

The Holy Spirit living inside of us empowers us to continue the supernatural ministry of Jesus on earth. This is our license to experience greater intimacy with God, press deeper into His Presence, and believe for the extraordinary works of John 14:12 to be released through our lives.

RECOMMENDED READING

Epistles to the Ephesians, Philippians, and Colossians
by the apostle Paul

Hosting the Presence by Bill Johnson

There is More by Randy Clark

The Glory Within by Corey Russell

Even Greater by Reinhard Bonnke

Greater Works by Smith Wigglesworth

Re-Think

~~

And when they could not come near Him
because of the crowd, they uncovered the
roof where He was. —Mark 2:4

22

SEE IMPOSSIBILITY FROM GOD'S PERSPECTIVE

~~

And do not be conformed to this world,
but be transformed by the renewing of
your mind. —ROMANS 12:2

Let us return to the account of the four men and their paralytic friend in Mark 2. At this point, things have gotten desperate for all of them. The situation was intensifying. The house was crowded and they could not get through the mob of people thronging to see Jesus. The place was so jam-packed that *"a crowd gathered, jamming the entrance so no one could get in or out"* (Mark 2:2 MSG). *No one.*

This is where we arrive at a crossroads. It is the following turn of events and choice of action on behalf of the four friends that birthed this entire book. Their response to the crowded house actually has life-changing implications for how we live our Christian lives today. It shows us one of the most important keys to exhibiting and sustaining breakthrough faith: *renewing our minds.*

Dallas Willard, one of my favorite Christian authors and a true prophetic voice to a generation, was not exaggerating about the importance of this subject when he wrote, "The prospering of God's cause on earth depends upon His people thinking well."[72] If we do not think well, primarily in regard to maintaining an accurate picture of the limitless God, the advancement of His Kingdom will be restrained. The breakthrough that these four men experienced for their friend had everything to do with them elevating their thinking and redefining the impossibility that was set before them.

THINK FROM GOD'S VANTAGE POINT

If then you were raised with Christ, seek those things which are above, where Christ is, sitting at the right hand of God. Set your mind on things above, not on things on the earth (Colossians 3:1-2).

What does it mean to experience a "renewed mind" (see Rom. 12:2) and set your "mind on things above"? It means that we see everything from God's point of view and live accordingly. The four men in Mark 2 made a choice to see their situation from God's perspective rather than a natural, limited mentality and experienced the miraculous as a result. The way we think determines what we see.

Some might respond, "I see where you are going with this, Larry. But what about Isaiah 55:8-9?" The familiar Scripture reads, *"'For My thoughts are not your thoughts, nor are your ways My ways,' says the Lord. 'For as the heavens are higher than the earth, so are My ways higher than your ways, and My thoughts than your thoughts.'"* This is absolutely true! God's thoughts and God's ways are infinitely higher and superior to ours. However, do these two verses in Isaiah 55 mean that the perspective and thought processes of God are inaccessible to everyday believers?

In Isaiah's day, yes, the thoughts of God were off-limits to everyday men and women. Things have shifted, though. In our day, the thoughts of God are accessible by normal believers. The wisdom of God is only an "ask" away (see James 1:5). This may sound absolutely wild to us, but think about it for a moment: the Spirit of Wisdom and Revelation, the Holy Spirit, now lives inside of each one of us (see Eph. 1:17). The blood of Jesus opened us up to a new way of living and, yes, a new way of thinking that was not accessible in the era of Isaiah under the Old Covenant.

God's thoughts *are* beyond ours—there is no question about it. But consider how Paul addresses this in First Corinthians 2. He reminds us that *"eye has not seen, nor ear heard, nor have entered into the heart of man the things which God has prepared for those who love Him"* (vs. 9). Some folks camp out on this verse without making the vital connection to the following passage: *"But God has revealed them to us through His Spirit. For the Spirit searches all things, yes, the deep things of God"* (vs. 10).

The way we think determines what we see.

Yes, what God has prepared for us is far beyond human ability to grasp, fathom, or imagine (see Eph. 3:20). However, the God who came up with the plans, and the same God who brings these supernatural plans to pass, now lives inside of us. This means we have access to His plans and we have access to His thoughts. Scripture tells us that we even have access to the *deep things of God*. The One who searches the depths of God lives within us. His name is Holy Spirit, and He is just as much God as the Father and the Son. The transition from verse 9 to 10 is designed to blow our minds. I think it does the job quite nicely.

TAKE ALL LIMITS OFF

With all of this in mind, it should be spiritually illegal for believers to place limitations on God in their thinking. If we place a ceiling upon God in how we think about Him, every roadblock and every hindrance we experience will be reason for us to make greater agreement with the deceptions we have entertained about God—namely, that He is unable to offer breakthrough in whatever situation we go through. *He is not limited*. To believe that God's ability and willingness are limited is entertaining an incorrect perspective about who God is.

Israel did this. Psalm 78:41 tells us that they *"limited the Holy One of Israel."* Remember, Israel's perspective did not change God at all; that is impossible. There is nothing we can do to change anything about God. Rather, they adjusted how *they* thought about God. They thought of Him as One with limitations, and, in turn, this perspective limited their *experience* of Him. They limited Him and responded to Him as though He was limited. If we place limitations on God in our thinking, it does nothing to Him; it also does *nothing for* us. If we are convinced that God can't, we won't. We won't believe. We won't press through. We won't persevere. We will not push for the impossible because we believe it is off-limits to Him; therefore, it will be off-limits to us.

If the four men thought of God as limited, they would have responded to the crowded house by turning around and going home, convinced that healing was not Jesus' will for their paralyzed friend. I would totally buy into the whole "God picks and chooses whom He wants to do a miracle for" type of system *if* the guys ended up breaking through the roof, and then Jesus said something like, "Didn't you take the hint? Didn't the crowded house deliver the message, loud and clear, that it was not My will to heal your friend?" Jesus did not say this however; He revealed the exact opposite. It is how Jesus responded in this account (and dozens more) that should change the way we think about God and take *every single limitation* off of Him.

> **It should be spiritually illegal for believers to place limitations on God in their thinking.**

The next verse in Psalm 78 offers some profound explanations on *how* the people of the time limited God: *"They did not remember His power"* (vs. 42). The psalm then goes on to list different supernatural exploits that God performed for them. We covered the need for testimony in three whole chapters because the topic is *that* important to releasing breakthrough faith. Remembering what God has done and keeping a record of His supernatural acts reminds us that there is truly no ceiling on the God of all power.

Going back to the four men and their paralyzed friend now: they demonstrated a perspective that took the limits off of God, quite the opposite of what we witness in Psalm 78. Sadly, too many of us today would simply embrace the crowded house as God's sovereign will and not press in for what God had really destined for us. When the house is crowded, we do not even consider going through the roof. That's just too far out there. That's wild thinking. That's fanatical. That's crazy. That's for "those *faith* people." If we are a believer in the Lord Jesus Christ, however, we are one of *those faith people.*

We need to stop agreeing with our circumstances. Let it be said of our generation that we broke through the roof of how we thought about God. He is without limits and this is how we should see Him. Rather than bringing Him down to our level of thinking, we have actually been invited to adopt *His* thoughts and perspectives about our situations. That is what it means to have a renewed mind. And this is what Paul was talking about when he invited us to *"set your mind on things above, not on things on the earth"* (Col. 3:2).

We are called to think like Christ. In fact, Paul also tells us that "the same mind" that was in Christ Jesus should be in us (see Phil. 2:5)! In First Corinthians 2:16 Paul presents a question, but then follows it up quickly with a bold answer: *"For 'who has known the mind of the Lord that he may instruct Him?" But we have the mind of Christ."* You have the mind of Christ! This reality is not only possible, but it is completely accessible because of the Holy Spirit who lives inside of us. He is the Spirit of Christ (see Rom. 8:9)!

Two key verses that confirm this are Romans 8:5: *"For those who live according to the flesh set their minds on the things of the flesh, but those who live according to the Spirit, the things of the Spirit,"* and Ephesians 4:23, where Paul urges us to *"be renewed in the spirit of your mind."* It is no coincidence that the man who had this revelation of the renewed mind was the same man who stepped into the dimension of extraordinary miracles (see Acts 19:11-12). Paul was able to walk in a breakthrough faith lifestyle because of his unlimited perspective of God. Paul did not have some mental picture of a God who was restrained and chained by natural impossibilities. He did not place limitations on the Almighty. His aim was to experience a continuous renewal of the mind so that moment by moment his thinking would come into greater agreement and alignment with who God truly was.

THE MIRACULOUS BECOMES NORMAL TO A RENEWED MIND

When we embrace Paul's perspective, miracles stop being the exception; they become the new normal. I am desperate to see a culture of believers rise up (and am currently seeing this in places across the earth), where miracles are standard practice for the Christian life. People in certain theological circles get bent out of shape because they think we are talking about miracles and the supernatural too much. You know why the subject is being overemphasized in certain places? It's because a foundational, normative element of Christianity—the continuous flow of God's supernatural Presence and power through everyday, Spirit-filled believers—has been marginalized for so long.

In the season of its resurgence, of course there is great emphasis. Yes, I agree that at times things can get slightly imbalanced. But understand that this emphasis is taking place because something that was basic to how Christianity was originally expressed is now being rediscovered. It is being unlocked by a people who recognize their inheritance of breakthrough faith. Breakthrough faith is the key that unlocks the supernatural lifestyle, and to operate in breakthrough faith our minds must be renewed to see God *as He is.*

> **Paul was able to walk in a breakthrough faith lifestyle because of his unlimited perspective of God.**

This is how the four friends saw Jesus that day. They looked at their friend's paralyzed condition and then looked back through the masses of people, surely to catch a glimpse of the One who could miraculously raise this man up. All it takes is a true glimpse of Jesus to awaken breakthrough faith and remove the ceiling on our limitations, obstacles, and impossibilities. The chasm between *what was the circumstance* and *what was possible* was not okay for them. They did not want to live in that place, as so many do today. Their paralyzed friend was lying before them while the solution to his affliction was just on the other side of the crowded sea of people.

Dallas Willard writes, "I realize that I will either allow my view of evil to determine my view of God and will cut Him down accordingly, or I will allow my view of God to determine my view of the evil and will elevate Him accordingly, accepting that nothing is beyond His power for good."[73] The four men did not redefine Jesus based on their circumstances, like many do today. They did not allow the evil circumstance that their friend was dealing with to ultimately shape their view of who Jesus was. This is poor thinking that produces lazy, destructive theology.

Rather, here is what they *did* do: these four men of faith elevated their thinking. Lazy theology looks at what's in front of us and assumes that some boundary or some obstacle is God's will by default. In Jonah's case, yes—the storm was God's merciful plan. In the paralytic's case, however, his infirmity was an ailment subject to the power of Jesus Christ. False theology would have reviewed the situation and concluded, "Well, I guess it's not God's will that our friend gets healed. After all, Jesus is there and we are here." Their elevated thinking is what fueled them to persevere and ultimately uncover the roof over Jesus. When this approach to God's will becomes common among believers, miracles will no longer be sporadic—they will become normative.

Willard also makes a profound statement concerning the ideas we entertain and the culture these ideas create in our lives: "One's culture is seen most clearly in what one thinks of as 'natural' and as requiring no explanation or even thought."[74] This is how I want us to start considering the supernatural and the miraculous. The supernatural must become natural. It is *natural* and *normal*, in that miracles, breakthroughs, signs, wonders, healings, deliverance, and impossible situations being turned around become characteristic of how Christianity is expressed.

It is never *common* in the sense that we treat miracles as routine or boring. Every breakthrough, from a broken finger being mended to someone being raised from the dead, deserves celebration. Every miracle heralds Kingdom advancement. Every breakthrough signifies that God's world is continuing to break into this one. As those who have inherited breakthrough faith, our definition of normal should be way different than what much of church culture is presently experiencing.

All it takes is a true glimpse of Jesus to awaken breakthrough faith and remove the ceiling on our limitations, obstacles, and impossibilities.

BREAK THROUGH YOUR ROOF

So what's the roof that you need to break through in your life? I want to take the final section of this chapter to talk with you, heart to heart. I want to get you thinking. I pray that everything we have talked about in regard to elevating your thinking and thinking from God's perspective helps you understand that when impossible situations present themselves to you, your initial response cannot be, "Well…that's just God's will."

This idea of removing a ceiling to receive our breakthrough, or release breakthrough for someone else, should not seem *out of the ordinary* for us. Removing ceilings and busting through rooftops is not unusual for the renewed mind. Removing the ceiling is simply a way of agreeing with God's will, no matter what is involved in the natural. Bill Johnson (who wrote a powerful guide on operating in the renewed mind, *Supernatural Power of a Transformed Mind*) explains, "We must go well beyond the Christian life we have known. We must redefine 'normal' Christianity so that it lines up with God's idea of normal, not the definition we have accepted and grown accustomed to based on our experiences (or lack thereof)."[75] This is where God wants to take us.

This is where He is calling all believers. He is extending an invitation for us: "Come up here" (see Rev. 4:1). The process begins in our minds.

> *Look up, and be alert to what is going on around Christ—that's where the action is. See things from His perspective* (Colossians 3:2 MSG).

Consider the circumstances you are facing today. Maybe you are personally doing all right, but you can think of a friend, family member, co-worker, or someone in school who is struggling with an impossible situation. Someone surely comes to mind. Sickness. Torment. Depression. Bondage. Addiction. A family situation in turmoil. Financial hardship. Fear. Anxiety. The list of possible situations is endless. Impossibility is not always a "raised from the dead" scenario—it is simply the thing we cannot get past in our own strength and ability. It demands divine intervention. Breakthrough faith is for anyone who has come as far as they can in their own strength and cannot make it any further. I want to help you stay in the race and get to the finish line. I want to help you become the person in your generation who presses in to actually see the other side of perseverance: *breakthrough!*

Removing ceilings and busting through rooftops is not unusual for the renewed mind.

This chapter leads us right into the closing section of the book. Here, we will discuss some of the practical things you need to know about walking in breakthrough faith—namely, the art of perseverance. Not quitting and not giving up. We cannot just "will up" this perspective; it is the result of a renewed mind. Breakthrough faith is sustained by the individual who keeps his or her mind in agreement with the Word of God and the realities of Heaven (see Col. 3:1-2).

Breakthrough faith comes before the actual breakthrough. If you are in the middle of actually receiving a breakthrough, you do not need faith. But if you are currently believing something that is in agreement with God's Word but it has not become a reality yet, you need faith.

POINT OF BREAKTHROUGH

To experience the miraculous life, where breakthrough faith is activated and released, we need to elevate our thinking to agree with God's. No limits, no boundaries.

~~~

RECOMMENDED READING

The Supernatural Power of a Transformed Mind by Bill Johnson

Renovation of the Heart by Dallas Willard

BREAK THROUGH

~~

So when they had broken through, they let down the bed on which the paralytic was lying. —MARK 2:4

23

PERSEVERE FOR THE PROMISE

~~~

*Be like those who stay the course with
committed faith and then get everything
promised to them.* —HEBREWS 6:12 MSG

*Multitudes will read comfortably about God's promises,
but you and I are called to possess the promises
and walk in them.* —FRANCIS FRANGIPANE[76]

It is easy to get stirred up talking about faith and breakthrough and miracles. Yet, when it comes to the topic of perseverance, it is often like a wet blanket. My prayer is that this chapter actually demolishes this false concept for us. I hope that as we catch the vision for what perseverance creates in *us*, we would begin celebrating what is happening behind the scenes during seasons of waiting and perseverance. The level of breakthrough God wants to release in, through, and to us is way beyond just one miracle or blessing. It is a lifestyle.

THE AVAILABILITY AND ACCESSIBILITY OF GOD'S KINGDOM PROVISION

First, we persevere with vision *because God's Kingdom provisions are available and accessible.* When we are insecure about what God's

Kingdom actually includes, it is tough to persevere for these promises. But we have a guarantee. Breakthrough is accessible! Jesus told us that the Kingdom of God was *at hand* (see Matt. 4:17). It is not somewhere out there. It is not off in outer space. Francis Frangipane notes that this truth of God's Kingdom being "at hand" means "that it is close enough to touch from where we are. Yet it must be fought for aggressively and attained with perseverance."[77] While we are not *guaranteed* to receive everything we ask for in the place of prayer, we do have a guarantee that everything we ask that is included in God's Kingdom agenda is *His will*.

DEALING WITH DISAPPOINTMENT AND DISCOURAGEMENT

Now that we know God's Kingdom provision is available and have gone to the Word to determine *what* this provision includes, we step into a realm that many fail to navigate correctly. This is the space between asking and receiving, between perseverance and promise. The enemy works overtime to destroy believers in this place. He knows that it is in this very space that he can cause us to give up, and in the process of giving up, redefine who God is for us.

We should be on constant guard against disappointment and discouragement. These two forces feed off one another. Disappointment happens when we start growing weary through impatience. Disappointment also happens—and more severely—when circumstances do not turn out the way Scripture promised they should. Disappointment happens when prayers appear like they went unanswered, when someone passed away, and when circumstances go from bad to worse. As a result, disappointment produces discouragement, which lives up to its very name. It disarms our courage. It robs us of the courage we need to persevere and actually break through the roof. It robs us of the very strength we need to sustain perseverance for the breakthrough.

What is the key to overcoming discouragement and disappointment? *It can only be found in fixing our eyes on the Unchanging One.* God's constancy is our desperate need during seasons of perseverance—especially when discouragement tries to set in and rob our zeal.

If God changes with our circumstances, we get lost. However, we are assured that no season or situation has the ability to change the Eternal One. Even though the disconnect between God's Word/God's nature and what actually happened can send us into major "God, I've got a question for You" mode, rest assured because He is not intimidated or angered by our questions. He welcomes them, actually. Questions reveal spiritual maturity, for the opposite of asking questions is going right into *experiential theology* mode. This is where we redefine who God is and what the Word says based on what happened in a specific situation. I would prefer to live out my entire life asking God questions and pressing in for answers, all the while believing that the Word is true, God is exactly who Scripture says He is, and the model of Jesus reveals Him accurately.

Francis Frangipane once again observes, "Discouragement comes when we look only at our circumstances without looking at the faithfulness and integrity of what God has promised."[78] Remember, faith does not deny circumstances. We do not try to pretend our problems away. However, if we are going to walk in perseverance, it is vital that we always see God as greater than the circumstances that we face. This will guide us through even the darkest valleys of disappointment.

> **God's constancy is our desperate need during seasons of perseverance.**

MY DAY WITH DISAPPOINTMENT

I lost a very, very dear friend to a brain tumor. In fact, he was among my *best* friends. What comes off as rather shocking is that my friend and his family exemplified breakthrough faith. They were praying for his healing. They were believing for the miraculous. They were standing in agreement. And what happened? He passed away. I was there. I was in the room shortly after his spirit departed from this world and went to be with the Lord.

How do we respond to moments like these? I was in absolute shock, quite honestly. I was upset. I was angry at the devil. I was confused with God. In my mind, what happened to him was downright illegal. As one can imagine, I was filled with all sorts of different feelings and emotions. But one thing I recognized throughout the whole process of pain was that I could not let my pain and questions for God and anger with the devil change my theology about God. My friend would not want this.

We need to mourn. We need to grieve. We need to feel everything that is appropriate, but then we need to rise up and keep pressing forward. Not abandoning memory, but pressing in for a greater demonstration of supernatural power in our lives.[79] I know that my dear friend is now among the great cloud of witnesses (see Heb. 12:1-2). He is looking down from Heaven, beckoning me—beckoning you, saying, "Do not quit." Do not get caught up in what happened, what didn't happen, or what should have happened. This is absolutely crippling to our perseverance.

Frangipane notes that the "enemy's specific goal is to get you to give up."[80] He knows what potential is on the other side of your perseverance. It is not just a miracle or breakthrough or blessing, but momentum. Miracles were always designed to carry momentum beyond you, beyond your church, and beyond your sphere of influence. When you experience breakthrough and start telling people about it, it stirs hunger in their hearts to experience more of God. Likewise, this hunger becomes contagious quickly, and the devil cannot afford to have a lot of God-hungry people causing problems for darkness.

At my friend's celebration of life, I had this unusual sense that he was in Heaven and actually cheering me onward. The last thing he would want is for us to stop believing God for the miraculous. His eyes now behold the overflowing storehouses of Heaven that are just waiting to be released into the earth. Why do they remain unaccessed then? Burned-out believers give up and end up settling for lives below their inheritance. They do not take advantage of all that is available to them. It is time to contend and fight for what is rightfully ours!

FIGHT FROM FAITH

We are not fighting our breakthroughs out of God's clenched hand; rather, we are fighting *from* what God has already provided *through* His hand. We are not fighting to get faith, but are fighting *from* a position of faith. Jesus explains this process in Matthew 11:12 as He describes this process, *"And from the days of John the Baptist until now the kingdom of heaven suffers violence, and the violent take it by force."*

Redeemed humanity has been called to enforce the Kingdom of God on earth, for we carry it inside of us (see Luke 17:21). Motivated by love and a desire to serve people, our vision is nothing short of a complete overthrow of darkness. However, the key to actually seeing darkness pushed back is taking our place as a persevering people rooted and grounded in God. We cannot let darkness push us into a corner; rather, we must become the restraining agent of darkness and push it back. This demands perseverance on our end because darkness fights back nasty, kicking and screaming.

Paul rightly encourages young Timothy to *"fight the good fight of faith"* (1 Tim. 6:12). Faith is a fight because of the demand for perseverance. To remain in an attitude of unwavering faith, we need unwavering focus on Jesus. This is what compelled the four men to bust through the ceiling and lower down their paralyzed friend before Jesus. Breaking through the ceiling signified that these guys were discontent living in the gulf between *what could be* and *what should be*. Knowledge that Jesus heals, in and of itself, does not produce breakthrough; rather, it is the dissatisfaction we feel because *what is* does not agree with *what should be*. This produces tenacity within us to climb up on a house, dig through the roof, and lower down our friend to experience the *what should be* of God's Kingdom.

> We are not fighting our breakthroughs out of God's clenched hand; rather, we are fighting *from* what God has already provided *through* His hand.

THE OTHER SIDE OF PERSEVERANCE

Now faith is the substance of things hoped for, the evidence of things not seen. For by it the elders obtained a good testimony (Hebrews 11:1-2).

What is on the other side of perseverance? *A good testimony.* You might think, "But what about…" and fill in the blank with the person who was prayed for or asked God for something, but it did not happen, or has not happened yet. We cannot ignore this. In fact, for every disappointment and every instance where the promise did not happen, we press on with increased intensity and vision. We do not beat ourselves up. We do not start playing the blame game. This is Christian maturity. It is persevering with questions, both answered and unanswered.

Why do we keep moving forward? We are compelled by what is possible and available on the other side of perseverance. Hebrews 11 gives us example after example of men and women who persevered for promises—*and received them.* In the same way that they obtained a *good testimony* by faith, the same is available for you and me.

LIVING IN SUSTAINED BREAKTHROUGH

Perseverance actually creates something in us—character. It builds patience. The fruit of the Spirit is cultivated. Remember, God does not send problems just to take us through the process. We must live mindful of what comes from whom. Does it come from God, or does it come from the enemy? If anything, us *embracing* the process and learning from it spits in the enemy's face. Through perseverance we are building the character fit to manage and carry sustained breakthrough.

When our perspective is like Peter and John, then we are ready. These two men possessed hearts that exemplified spiritual growth and maturity. They were not perfect by any means, but they demonstrated the ability to carry a breakthrough lifestyle with integrity. Read their account below:

Now Peter and John went up together to the temple at the hour of prayer, the ninth hour. And a certain man lame from his mother's womb was carried, whom they laid daily at the gate of the temple which is called Beautiful, to ask alms from those who entered the temple; who, seeing Peter and John about to go into the temple, asked for alms. And fixing his eyes on him, with John, Peter said, "Look at us." So he gave them his attention, expecting to receive something from them. Then Peter said, "Silver and gold I do not have, but what I do have I give you: In the name of Jesus Christ of Nazareth, rise up and walk." And he took him by the right hand and lifted him up, and immediately his feet and ankle bones received strength. So he, leaping up, stood and walked and entered the temple with them—walking, leaping, and praising God. And all the people saw him walking and praising God. Then they knew that it was he who sat begging alms at the Beautiful Gate of the temple; and they were filled with wonder and amazement at what had happened to him (Acts 3:1-10).

This is what we all want, right? We want the miracle. We want the impossible situation turned around. We want the broken thing fixed. We want the crooked thing straightened. We want the marriage restored. We want the cancer healed. We want our children serving God. We read miracle accounts like this and think to ourselves, "Yes, this is what I want, God!"

Through perseverance we are building the character fit to manage and carry sustained breakthrough.

God actually desires this activity more than we do. He wants it in both greater quantity and greater quality than we can possibly imagine. If this were not so, Jesus would not have given us the harrowing invitation into a lifestyle of greater works. So what positioned the early church to walk in this consistent, sustained expression of breakthrough faith and corresponding miracles?

Jump back into the Acts 3 account and find out:

> *Now as the lame man who was healed held on to Peter and John, all the people ran together to them in the porch which is called Solomon's, greatly amazed. So when Peter saw it, he responded to the people: "Men of Israel, why do you marvel at this? Or why look so intently at us, as though by our own power or godliness we had made this man walk? The God of Abraham, Isaac, and Jacob, the God of our fathers, glorified His Servant Jesus, whom you delivered up and denied in the presence of Pilate, when he was determined to let Him go. But you denied the Holy One and the Just, and asked for a murderer to be granted to you, and killed the Prince of life, whom God raised from the dead, of which we are witnesses* (Acts 3:11-15).

First, when it came time to testify, Peter gave the right answer: *he redirected focus to God, off himself, and off the miracle.* God is seeking the generation who is desperate for an explosion of the miraculous because they are fit to steward breakthrough correctly. When God supernaturally turns a situation around, these "stewards of breakthrough" are intentional about celebrating the miracle but glorifying the Miracle Maker even more. They refuse to become "God's people of power for the hour," acting as if their ability had anything to do with the miracle. God's glory is front and center of every miracle!

Secondly, Peter sees evangelistic potential in the miracle, noting that it was by faith in Jesus' name that the man was healed: *"And His name, through faith in His name, has made this man strong, whom you see and know. Yes, the faith which comes through Him has given him this perfect soundness in the presence of you all"* (Acts 3:16). Immediately after linking the miracle to faith in the name of Jesus—demonstrating the Savior's authority and supremacy—Peter goes right into an appeal for those who witnessed the miracle to *"repent therefore and be converted, that your sins may be blotted out, so that times of refreshing may come from the presence of the Lord"* (Acts 3:19).

Third, *miracles produce momentum.* After Peter shares the Gospel, two things happen. In Acts 4:1-3 we see that the religious leaders got very upset that the name of Jesus was being preached. As a result, they seized Peter and John, and held them in custody. We *know* that Peter and John stewarded the miracle well because of what happened next. The second thing we notice is that even though the two guys are out of the picture, the miracle itself still produces a harvest: *"But many of those who heard the message believed (adhered to and trusted in and relied on Jesus as the Christ). And their number grew and came to about 5,000"* (Acts 4:4 AMP). The miracle and the message produced a momentum that brought roughly 5,000 people into the Kingdom.

God's glory is front and center of every miracle!

Just imagine what becomes possible when every single believer starts exercising breakthrough faith *like this*? Truly, the Desire of All Nations will be exalted and, in turn, the masses will turn to Christ. This is what empowers us to sustain breakthrough rather than experience a sporadic miracle here and there. When it becomes all about Jesus, the One whom all the signs and wonders point to, perseverance becomes less problematic. It is one thing to try and persevere, clinging to a promise. However, when we know the character of the One making the promises and are intent on seeing Him receive all the glory when His promises come to pass, we will not back down. We will not give up. Our aim will be to model those described in Hebrews 11:2, who through faith obtained a *good* testimony.

POINT OF BREAKTHROUGH

Perseverance is our key to walking in breakthrough; the miracle we are praying and believing for is on the other side of perseverance. Giving up cannot be an option!

～～

RECOMMENDED READING

This Day We Fight by Francis Frangipane

24

KEYS TO LIVING OUT BREAKTHROUGH FAITH

～～～

So also faith, if it does not have works (deeds and actions of obedience to back it up), by itself is destitute of power (inoperative, dead).—JAMES 2:17 AMP

When I think of people who pushed Christianity out of stationary mode and toward active, living, working faith, John Wimber immediately comes to mind. He was a key leader in the Association of Vineyard Churches movement during the 1980s and beyond.

I believe that God is not looking for squeaky-clean, pitch-perfect people to demonstrate His power through. Wimber personifies this. When he first encountered God and gave his life to Christ, he was a "beer-guzzling, drug-abusing pop musician, who was converted at the age of 29 while chain-smoking his way through a Quaker-led Bible study."[81] And yet, in his first ten years of being a believer, he led hundreds of people to Jesus. He was a passionate evangelist for the Kingdom! But he still saw a gulf between what was revealed in Scripture and what believers were experiencing in their everyday lives.

When Wimber read the Bible, he saw examples of Jesus and the early church "doing the stuff"—the "stuff" referring to moving in power, miracles, signs, wonders, healing, and the prophetic. This became his desire. If supernatural breakthrough was common in the early church, why was it being ignored *today*? Wimber's legacy is outstanding. A man of great humility, wisdom, and power, one of the great contributions he made to the furtherance of modern Christianity is showing that it is biblically legal for *all* believers to extend their faith and walk in supernatural power. Just knowing it on the page was not sufficient for Wimber, and it should not be enough for us either. This man placed a demand on what was revealed in Scripture and proceeded to shift the landscape of how Christianity is expressed. This is truly the *faith in action* that we read about in James 2.

Demons know what the Bible says. They believe in one God (see James 2:19). And this is why they tremble. It should not be enough for us to see the demons tremble but still continue to bring terror and destruction to countless lives. We should desire to see them destroyed (see 1 John 3:8). Every demon should be served a notice of eviction. The enemy is not afraid of people who believe in God; he is absolutely terrified of those who believe that God lives inside of them, and live accordingly.

James 2:17 is the classic *"faith without works is dead"* passage. The Message Bible puts it this way, which is highly relevant for our subject matter: *"Isn't it obvious that God-talk without God-acts is outrageous nonsense?"* I do not want to give you a book full of spiritual-sounding God-talk. I want to equip you to actually do the God-acts.

In James 2:14 we read: *"Dear friends, do you think you'll get anywhere in this if you learn all the right words but never do anything? Does merely talking about faith indicate that a person really has it?"* (MSG). Talking or learning about faith does not profit us at all *unless* we put the principles into practice. This is how we will finish up our journey together!

PRACTICAL STEPS TO WALKING OUT OUR FAITH

Every chapter has been leading up to this point in the book. I am going to now share some practical tips on *how* to effectively walk out this breakthrough faith lifestyle.

Pursue a lifestyle of biblical holiness. This is the first and most foundational key to living a life of sustained breakthrough faith. Does holiness mean that in order for you to receive a miracle or breakthrough, you need to be absolutely 100% perfect? Of course not. However, in our twenty-first century church culture, I fear we have lost the weight and preciousness of holiness. It's not restrictive, it's beautiful. Why? Peter reminds us of how relevant this call to holiness is for Christians today: For the Scriptures say, *"You must be holy because I am holy"* (1 Pet. 1:16). People may read a verse like this and groan, focusing on the *you must be holy* part. This is because we are not seeing the entire passage in context. God is actually inviting us to model His nature on Earth. We are invited to imitate the very character of God—the one Who ransomed us, redeemed us, and loves us with an everlasting love. I spent so much time earlier in the book talking about imitating God because that is, ultimately, what holiness is. We are imitating God in every way through the empowering presence of the Spirit. Our words. Our thoughts. Our actions. What we set before our eyes and ears. How we carry ourselves. The company we keep. By default, every area of our lives will be impacted when our delight and desire is to imitate God.

I'm sure that when I use the word *holiness*, different images are coming to your mind. Perhaps you envision legalistic church communities, where the main emphasis is what you can*not* do instead of what you can do. Rules. Regulations. Restrictions. Sour faces. This is another ditch people have fallen into over the years. Holiness does not begin with our moral codes or religious regulations—it begins with a heart that simply says "Yes, God—I want to imitate your ways and nature because I love who You are." Love is cultivated in intimacy, and intimacy produces imitation. Holiness is a lifestyle committed to imitating God. The powerful flipside is that holiness and breakthrough faith come from the same posture of heart. Jesus never gave us an "and/or" reality, where we had to select either holiness *or* power. We get to walk in both! The Spirit who conforms us into the image of Jesus in our character is the same Spirit who empowers us to represent Jesus in supernatural demonstration.

Here is the bottom line: We cannot live in sin and expect to walk out a lifestyle of victory and breakthrough. We cannot pursue the "power, signs, wonders, and miracles" part of God, while leaving the character, integrity, morality, Beatitudes and fruit of the Spirit alone. Imitating God means we joyfully say "Yes" to representing Jesus in every way on Earth—in both purity and power.

Choose your company carefully: This includes close friends and, most importantly, your significant other. These are the people who have speaking-power in your life. In other words, what they say to you and over you tends to impact how you believe or how you think. Bible teacher Marilyn Hickey delivered a fantastic message on the importance of having four radical-faith friends—based on the account in Mark 2.[82] I can say without a doubt that I am where I am today because I have intentionally surrounded myself with people of *"like precious faith"* (see 2 Pet. 1:1). It is important to identify these people in your life. As for my significant other, my wife constantly challenges me to take God at His Word and live like it is true.

> **The enemy is not afraid of people who believe in God; he is absolutely terrified of those who believe that God lives inside of them, and live accordingly.**

In college, I so fondly remember gathering around the apartment coffee table with my two closest friends in the world, and praying through the impossible. Encouraging each other through struggles. Worshipping through worry. We did not deny that problems existed; we openly discussed them. At the same time, we made a decision to *respond* to them with an elevated perspective. These guys helped me maintain the mind of Christ in the midst of all kinds of craziness—from dating dilemmas to professors suffering disease to persevering in our relationships with Jesus. Regardless of the seasons we went through together, I could always count on their words to awaken my faith rather than discourage it. The desire for the impossible was written in their DNA.

There was no request too outlandish or too off-limits to bring before the Holy One.

Of course, not all of our friends and acquaintances can be people of like precious faith; in fact, many should be those who either do not know the Lord yet or are still maturing in their walk. These are the people we *freely give* to, helping them develop into the mighty men and women God has destined them to be. However, when it comes to the people who are closest to us, and the ones who are consistently influencing our lives, it is vital they are people who feed our faith and push us toward the impossible.

Here are some benefits of radical-faith friends:

- They call your thinking up higher to agree with God, not downward to agree with the issues and problems you face.

- They encourage you, even through the dark seasons, by keeping your focus on the greatness and ability of God, while also being sensitive to the struggle.

- They help you feed on God's faithfulness by sharing testimony of how God is moving—they focus on what He is doing, not what He is *not doing*.

Find testimonies of what God is doing: Watch them. Listen to them. Read them. Feed yourself on the faithfulness of God through testimony (see Ps. 37:3). Remember, the four friends came to the place where Jesus was because of what they *heard*. Testimony brought them out of the woodwork and awakened faith within them—faith that ultimately broke through a ceiling and experienced the miraculous. It is vital for the health of our faith to constantly be focused on what God *is* doing.

So let us get practical for a moment. How can we do this on an everyday level?

If you are a reader, I encourage you to read biographies of the men and women who experienced supernatural breakthrough as normative. Examples include Kathryn Kuhlman, Smith Wigglesworth (*Ever*

Increasing Faith, Even Greater), John G. Lake (*Complete Collection of His Teachings*), Tommy Welchel's *True Stories of the Miracles of Azusa Street and Beyond,* and many others.

If you prefer video, go on YouTube and find reliable testimonies of people who have received God's miracles in powerful ways.

If you know of people who have experienced God's supernatural power and appear to walk in this breakthrough faith, connect with them. If mentorship is possible, ask them to take you under their wing and share their stories. Even if you just get together for coffee or lunch, it is vital for us to encourage each other, sharing testimony of what God is doing.

It is vital for the health of our faith to constantly be focused on what God *is* doing.

"Soak" or rest in God's Presence: The "soaking" language might sound a bit out there to some people. Also, for some type A personalities, just "resting" in the Presence of God is quite the outlandish thought. "So, how does this whole soaking thing work?" That is a fun one to explain. "Well, you just kind of sit there and do...*nothing.* Just rest in God." I can just hear the responses: "Okay...so what do I do while I am resting in God?" That's me, for sure.

Do you know why it is so important for us to learn how to rest in God? It is not so much that we sit around and do nothing, but we are learning how to live from a perspective of rest. His Presence is a vital catalyst to sustaining this rest in our lives. Rest is the most powerful posture we can assume when activating breakthrough faith. We do not generate faith. Our willpower does not muster it up. Our striving and pressing and worry and struggle do nothing to create faith. So what is the key? Rest. We must recognize that we cannot do anything about the situation. We cannot move the impossible circumstance.

However, we are entrusting the impossible to the One who is both able and willing to work as we rest. Rest demonstrates trust, and trust fuels faith. Trust is only built through intimacy. This is why we devoted such a strong emphasis to the knowledge of God in the previous chapters.

"Soaking" or resting in God's Presence is a powerful statement of trust. We are physically choosing to do nothing *except* focus on Him, trusting that He is moving behind the scenes.

Declare God's Word: We must understand there are two aspects of declaration. Many of us are familiar with Option 1—confessing Scripture. This is important. Does our confession do anything to God? Not really. It does, however, keep what we say in agreement with what God says and what God thinks. And here is Option 2—saying what the Father is saying. This is beyond just quoting a Bible verse. Sometimes we quote a Scripture but other times we have to command a spirit to leave. Sometimes we recount a Bible verse and other times we rebuke a disease.

What we read in Scripture serves as the basis for saying what the Father is saying, but again, it is not simply quoting a Bible verse. The ability to do this comes from intimacy with the Father. When we know that torment and bondage is not God's will, we simply declare, "No, in Jesus' name!" When we are entertaining thoughts that have the potential to steal, kill, or destroy, we already know God's heart on the matter. We simply need to say, "Enough—go, in Jesus' name!" This releases the commanding power of God. Remember, His words are *spirit and life*. We are not commanding God to do anything. Rather, we are saying what God would say about the circumstance that we are up against.

Carry others to the place of breakthrough using your faith: Did you know that your faith can actually bring someone else into a breakthrough—even if they do not necessarily have faith for themselves? I am not presenting any type of principle or ironclad rule here. All I know is that in Mark 2:3 we see that the paralytic's four friends carried him to receive his miracle. Obviously, they were full of faith because they were the ones who broke through the roof and lowered their friend down to Jesus. I would encourage you to find people whom you can *carry* using your faith.

Rest is the most powerful posture we can assume when activating breakthrough faith.

Never underestimate your role as an intercessor. I can list time after time and story after story where God supernaturally transformed situations for people by using others to carry them to victory.

Also, never underestimate the power of persevering on behalf of someone whose faith is struggling, or taking it a step further, someone who might have no faith at all! Even then God is still faithful. This is really the heart of the *breakthrough faith* message. It is not about us only receiving *our* breakthrough; it is about living a life of sustained victory so that we can carry others into an encounter with God's supernatural power. No, we cannot carry the weight of the world on our shoulders. Someone cannot have a relationship with God *through* us. Rather, carrying someone to the place of breakthrough would be akin to intercessory prayer.

Keep Jesus as the main focus. We conclude with the most important focus of all—*Jesus Christ.* It is easy to get caught up in miracles, signs, and wonders. Some people end up getting so focused on putting the correct faith principles to work and pressing in to get what they need from God, that they forget the point of it all.

Did you know that it is possible to miss God's invitation to relationship in the midst of miracles? Israel did this time after time. Scripture tells us that they continuously witnessed God's miraculous acts, but their hearts were still disconnected from Him. They did not have eyes to see where the signs were pointing.

In John 6:26 Jesus makes a stunning comment, *"I tell you the truth, you want to be with Me because I fed you, not because you understood the miraculous signs"* (NLT). When we understand what miraculous signs are purposed to do, we celebrate the breakthrough and then *desire* to be with Jesus, the author and finisher of our faith. He is our focus. He is our emphasis. He is the center. He is not a side topic. He is not a formula that we use to grab a blessing and then tip our hat to God. His name is not some magic word that we use to get what we want out of God. He's not a celestial Santa Claus or divine vending machine. He is the Lord of Heaven and earth. Every sign points to Jesus. Every wonder stirs up our awe and holy fear toward the Savior.

CONCLUSION

Everything I write and speak about is motivated by the following statement: What one generation experiences as an outpouring or revival, the next should walk in as a lifestyle. As we experience a "faith revival," something is being expected of us. The Holy Spirit is issuing a glorious summons to everyone who has an ear to hear. Walking in breakthrough faith should never end with us; if anything, it starts with us and will only increase in momentum and power as future generations emerge on to the scene.

In order for them to know how to walk out this faith, we need to pass on the message. More than just reading a book, my prayer is that this message would be vividly displayed through your life.

This will be written for the generation to come, that a people yet to be created may praise the Lord (Psalm 102:18).

Afterword

RECEIVE BREAKTHROUGH FAITH TODAY

~~

*For by grace you have been saved through faith,
and that not of yourselves; it is the gift of God,
not of works, lest anyone should boast. For we
are His workmanship, created in Christ Jesus for
good works, which God prepared beforehand that
we should walk in them.* —EPHESIANS 2:8-10

I celebrate the miracles, signs, and wonders that a life of breakthrough faith produces—otherwise, I would not have written this book. My prayer over this project is that the body of Christ would begin to walk out a lifestyle of consistent supernatural power, not just occasional victory. But to what end? I want to see Jesus Christ high and lifted up so that all would know He is the one true God. He is the only way to eternal salvation. And He is our invitation to a life of purpose and significance here on earth.

Jesus is alive.

He is not a concept.

He is not one among many gods.

Jesus is God.

There is no other name under Heaven by which man can be saved from sin.

Jesus is the Savior.

By nature, mankind is sinful.

Our natural bent is toward sin and rebellion.

We could not save ourselves from this drive toward evil tendencies.

We were incapable of becoming right with God.

This is why God Himself came to the earth as Jesus Christ.

He lived the life that you and I could never live—one of absolute perfection.

He died the death that you and I deserved to die—and even if we had died this same death, our humanness would have prevented our sacrifice from doing anything about the sin problem.

Jesus' blood was perfect and holy and sinless—it purchased forgiveness for your sin and my sin. For the sins of the entire world. All of the wrong. All of the rebellion. All of the pride. All of the anger. All of the lust. All of the hatred. Every thought, action, and attitude in rebellion toward God was taken care of at the cross.

We simply need to receive this free gift that God provided through Jesus. *This is how we receive breakthrough faith!* If you have already made Jesus Christ your Lord and Savior, I have good news for you: you already have breakthrough faith living inside of you. However, if you have never invited Jesus to come into your heart, forgive your sins, give you a fresh start, and fill you with the Holy Spirit to live out the supernatural lifestyle we just explored, I want to give you the opportunity right here, right now. It is so simple. You can just pray with me:

Jesus, thank You for living a perfect life. I couldn't do it.

Thank You, Jesus, for dying the perfect death, offering complete forgiveness for my sins.

Father, I confess that my sin, my wrong, my rebellion—it all deserves death, for the Bible says that the soul that sins shall die.

This is what causes me to feel unworthy before You, the Holy God. But I don't need to stay this way. You made it possible for me to stand righteous before You!

Thank You, Jesus, for taking my place and dying the death that I deserved. You took upon yourself all of my sin—past, present, and future.

I am forgiven. I am clean. I am shameless. I am guilt-free. Thank You, Jesus.

And finally, thank You for filling me with Your Holy Spirit. You forgave my sin so that I could spend eternity in Heaven with You, but also so that I could be filled with Your Presence and power here on earth. I want to see Your Kingdom bring freedom, healing, and breakthrough so that all would know that Jesus Christ is alive!

If you prayed this simple prayer, I believe the Holy Spirit performed an utterly supernatural work in your heart. Jesus Christ saved you from your sin, made you a child of God, and filled you with the Holy Spirit. You are now what they call "born again." You are a Christian. You have a room reserved in Heaven and are empowered with breakthrough faith for your mission on earth. I would love to hear from you. My ministry information is listed in the back of this book. I want to do what I can to help you transition beyond a one-time prayer and start living out this supernatural Christian life. *It is your inheritance!*

Above all, I pray that every breakthrough you experience fuels your passion and pursuit for this Jesus, to know Him more, to worship Him more deeply, and to boldly declare His glorious Gospel to the nations, starting with your own sphere of influence.

ENDNOTES

1. If you are not yet a believer in the Lord Jesus Christ, I would encourage you to immediately flip to the Afterword in the back of the book to read more about how to make this glorious, life-changing decision.
2. Kris Vallotton, *Heavy Rain* (Ventura, CA: Regal, 2010), 65.
3. Jack Graham, *Unseen* (Grand Rapids, MI: Bethany House, 2013), 37.
4. A.W. Tozer, *God's Greatest Gift to Man.*
5. Francis Frangipane, *This Day We Fight* (Grand Rapids, MI: Chosen, 2005), 21.
6. Martin H. Manser, *The Westminster Collection of Christian Quotations* (Louisville, KY: Westminster John Knox Press, 2001), 390.
7. C.S. Lewis, *The Screwtape Letters.*
8. Perry Stone, *Exposing Satan's Playbook* (Lake Mark: Charisma House, 2012), 153.
9. Ibid.
10. Ibid.
11. Wayne Grudem, *Systematic Theology* (Grand Rapids, MI: Zondervan), 414.
12. A.W. Tozer, *Set of the Sail* (Harp Hill: WingSpread Publishers, 1986), 28.
13. Neil T. Anderson, *The Bondage Breaker* (Eugene, OR: Harvest House Publishers, 1990).
14. Bill Johnson, *Hosting the Presence* (Shippensburg, PA: Destiny Image, 2012), 34.

15. Wayne Grudem, *Systematic Theology* (Grand Rapids, MI: Zondervan), 412.

16. Martin Luther, "A Mighty Fortress is Our God."

17. A.W. Tozer, *Set of the Sail* (Harp Hill: WingSpread Publishers, 1986), 27.

18. Adapted from Allen Hood's "Revival" sermon at Harbour Church in Pompano Beach, FL. 2008.

19. Dallas Willard, *Renovation of the Heart* (Colorado Springs: NavPress, 2002), 103.

20. A. W. Tozer, *The Knowledge of the Holy* (New York, NY: HarperSanFrancisco, 1992), 43.

21. Joyce Meyer, *Knowing God Intimately* (New York: Warner Faith, 2003), 123.

22. Bill Johnson, *Dreaming With God* (Shippensburg, PA: Destiny Image, 2006), 27.

23. R. Loren Sanford, "A New Move of God Is Emerging," Charisma News, September 7, 2013, http://www.charismanews.com/opinion/40852-a-new-move-of-god-is-emerging (accessed September 9, 2013).

24. Bill Johnson, *Hosting the Presence* (Shippensburg, PA: Destiny Image, 2012), 25.

25. For contemporary works on the Holy Spirit I would recommend *Holy Spirit* by John Bevere, *The God I Never Knew* by Robert Morris, *Holy Fire* by R.T. Kendall, and *Forgotten God* by Francis Chan. For classic works I would recommend *The Person and the Work of the Holy Spirit* by R.A. Torrey, *Experiencing the Holy Spirit* by Andrew Murray, and *Mystery of the Holy Spirit* by A.W. Tozer.

26. F.F. Bosworth, *Christ the Healer* (Grand Rapids, MI: Chosen Books, 2000), 50.

27. Leonard, Ravenhill, "We Must Demonstrate Christianity," Leonard's Ravenhill's Ministry: Quotes Archive, http://www.leonard-ravenhill.com/category/quotes (accessed February 12, 2014).

28. Gregory Boyd and Paul Eddy, *Across the Spectrum* (Grand Rapids: Baker Academic, 2009), 236.

29. Paul Brandeis Raushenbush, "Atonement and the Wrath of God: The Great Hymn Debate Widens," *The Huffington Post*, August 18, 2013, http://www.huffingtonpost.com/2013/08/18/hymn-wrath-of -god-_n_3775498.html.

30. F.F. Bosworth, *Christ the Healer* (Grand Rapids: Chosen Books, 2000), 50.

31. N.T. Wright, *Surprised By Hope* (New York: HarperCollins, 2008), 201.

32. Tullian Tchividjian, *Unfashionable* (Colorado Springs: Multnomah, 2009), 57.

33. Dallas Willard, *Renovation of the Heart* (Colorado Springs: NavPress, 2002), 87.

34. Timothy J. Keller, *The Reason for God* (New York, NY: Riverhead Books, 2009), 93.

35. Randy Clark, *There is More* (Bloomington: Chosen Books, 2013), 103.

36. For books that provide solid teaching on the healing gifts of the Holy Spirit, I strongly recommend Reinhard Bonnke's *Taking Action* and Derek Prince's *Gifts of the Holy Spirit*.

37. Graham Twelftree, *In the Name of Jesus* (Grand Rapids, MI: Baker Academic, 2007), 140.

38. Francis MacNutt, *Deliverance From Evil Spirits* (Grand Rapids, MI: Chosen Books, 2009), 71.

39. Kris Vallotton, *Spirit Wars* (Bloomington: Chosen Books, 2012), 178.

40. This is a revelation Corey has shared repeatedly when speaking.

41. Billy Graham, "What is Faith?" *The Prayer Life*, http://www .theprayerlife.com/What%20is%20Faith-Billy%20Graham.html (accessed October 8, 2013).

42. Fred and Sharon Wright, *World's Greatest Revivals* (Shippensburg, PA: Destiny Image, 2007), 95.

43. Wesley Duewel, *Revival Fire* (Grand Rapids, MI: Zondervan, 1995), 77.

44. Eddie L. Hyatt, *2000 Years of Charismatic Christianity* (Lake Mark: Charisma House, 2002), 109.

45. Nancy Gibbs & Richard N. Ostling, "God's Billy Pulpit," *Time*, November 15, 1993 http://www.time.com (accessed October 8, 2013).

46. Ibid.

47. Settle, Gary, (February 22, 1976). "Kathryn Kuhlman, Evangelist And Faith Healer, Dies in Tulsa," *New York Times*.

48. Roberts Liardon, *Kathryn Kuhlman: A Spiritual Biography of God's Miracle Worker* (New Kensington: Whitaker House, 2005), 57.

49. Andrew Wommack, "The Faith of God," Andrew Wommack Ministries, http://www.awmi.net/extra/article/faith_god (accessed October 8, 2013).

50. Michael J. Klassen, *Strange Fire, Holy Fire* (Minneapolis: Bethany House, 2009), 149-150.

51. "Potential & Kinetic Energy," Energy Education, http://www .energyeducation.tx.gov/energy/section_1/topics/potential_and _kinetic_energy/ (accessed February 11, 2014).

52. Wesley Duewel, *Revival Fire* (Grand Rapids, MI: Zondervan, 1995), 204.

53. Allan Anderson, *An Introduction to Pentecostalism* (New York: Cambridge University Press, 2004), 40.

54. Wesley Duewel, *Revival Fire* (Grand Rapids, MI: Zondervan, 1995), 204.

55. Bill Johnson, *Release the Power of Jesus* (Shippensburg, PA: Destiny Image, 2009), 36.

56. Charles H. Spurgeon, "The Story of God's Mighty Acts," The Spurgeon Archive, http://www.spurgeon.org/sermons/0263.htm (accessed October 22, 2013).

57. Mark Miller, *Experiential Storytelling* (Grand Rapids, MI: Zondervan, 2003), 30.

58. Bill Johnson and Randy Clark, *The Essential Guide to Healing* (Minneapolis, MN: Chosen, 2011), 169.

59. Check out Delia Knox's powerful testimony here, for her first time walking in twenty-two years: http://www.youtube.com/ watch?v=Y1YxJfLKF7c.

60. Bill Johnson and Randy Clark, *The Essential Guide to Healing* (Minneapolis, MN: Chosen, 2011), 161.

61. Charles H. Spurgeon, "The Story of God's Mighty Acts," The Spurgeon Archive, http://www.spurgeon.org/sermons/0263.htm (accessed October 22, 2013).

62. Bill Johnson and Randy Clark, *The Essential Guide to Healing* (Minneapolis, MN: Chosen, 2011), 169.

63. Charles H. Spurgeon, "The Story of God's Mighty Acts," The Spurgeon Archive, http://www.spurgeon.org/sermons/0263.htm (accessed October 22, 2013).

64. Bill Johnson and Randy Clark, *The Essential Guide to Healing* (Minneapolis, MN: Chosen, 2011), 161.

65. Charles H. Spurgeon, "The Story of God's Mighty Acts," The Spurgeon Archive, http://www.spurgeon.org/sermons/0263.htm (accessed on October 22, 2013).

66. Charles H. Spurgeon, "The Story of God's Mighty Acts," The Spurgeon Archive, http://www.spurgeon.org/sermons/0263.htm (accessed on October 22, 2013).

67. A.W. Tozer, "How To Be Filled with the Holy Spirit" (Martino Fine Books, 2010).

68. Sam Storms, *Pleasures Forevermore* (Colorado Springs: NavPress, 2000), 140.

69. A.W. Tozer, *Experiencing the Presence of God* (Ventura, CA: Regal, 2010), 81.

70. A.W. Tozer, *Rut, Rot or Revival* (Camp Hill, PA: Wingspread Publishers, 1993), 9.

71. Larry Sparks, "3 Ways to Unlock the Supernatural in Your Life," *Charisma Magazine*, October 8, 2013, http://www.charismamag.com/spirit/revival/18901-3-ways-to-unlock-the-supernatural-in-your-life.

72. Dallas Willard, *Renovation of the Heart* (Colorado Springs: NavPress, 2002), 105.

73. Ibid., 109-110.

74. Ibid., 97.

75. Bill Johnson, *Supernatural Power of a Transformed Mind* (Shippensburg, PA: Destiny Image, 2005), 31.

76. Francis Frangipane, *This Day We Fight* (Grand Rapids, MI: Chosen, 2005), 9. By the way, this book is outstanding and is a perfect accompaniment for this chapter.

77. Ibid., 8.

78. Ibid., 60.

79. Chris Gore covers this topic exceptionally in his book *Walking in Supernatural Healing Power* (Shippensburg, PA: Destiny Image, 2014).

80. Frangipane, *This Day We Fight*, 9.

81. *Christianity Today*, editorial, February 9, 1998.
82. Check out Marilyn Hickey's message "Four Crazy Faith Friends" at http://secure.marilynandsarah.org/p-325-four-crazy-faith-friends.aspx.

ABOUT THE AUTHOR

Larry Sparks is on a mission that can be captured in three words: Encounter, Activate, and Transform. His driving passion is to see people encounter the presence of the Holy Spirit, activate God's power in their everyday lives through supernatural discipleship, and transform their worlds by representing Jesus Christ and advancing His Kingdom.

As an author, speaker, and revivalist, Larry is committed to harnessing the power of media to equip the body of Christ for supernatural living. His ministry, Equip Culture, exists to provide tools and resources that empower Christians to discover their inheritance in Christ and live a life where anything is possible.

Larry's approach to ministry combines the clear, practical teaching of Scripture with the power of the Holy Spirit. He graduated from Palm Beach Atlantic University with a B.A. in Screenwriting and Communications. Presently, he is pursuing graduate theological studies at Regent University in Virginia Beach (MDiv, Christian Theology).

Supernatural discipleship is one of Larry's main areas of emphasis. He presently serves as Director of Curriculum Resources for Destiny Image Publishers where he creates media-based resources that equip believers to sustain supernatural lifestyles characterized by the pursuit of God's presence and demonstration of the gifts of the Holy Spirit, signs, wonders, and miracles.

Having ministered in university, church, and conference settings, Larry delivers a message of supernatural empowerment and spiritual passion. A repeat guest on CBN's Spiritual Gifts Webcast and host of the weekly Voice of Destiny radio broadcast, he is also a blogger, columnist and a regular contributor to Charisma Magazine and Charisma News.

Subscribe to Larry's blog at www.lawrencesparks.com

Follow Larry on Twitter @LarryVSparks